PEBBLES IN THE RICE: MY LIFE IN IRAN

LISA J. RADCLIFFE

Pebbles in the Rice

© 2016 Lisa J. Radcliffe

ISBN: 978-1-66780-688-4

eBook ISBN 13: 978-1-51463-890-3

CONTENTS

Prologue 1

Chapter 1:
Unplanned Visitors.. 5

Chapter 2
The Making of the Radcliffes............................... 14

Chapter 3
Unanticipated Courtship 19

Chapter 4
Homecoming 33

Chapter 5
Getting Acquainted 39

Chapter 6
Student of Culture 52

Chapter 7
Who's in Charge Now?... 63

Chapter 8
In Black and White 68

Chapter 9
Spreading the Truth 74

Chapter 10
Returning Home 80

Chapter 11
Finding Happiness Among Fifth-Graders.......... 85

Chapter 12
The Complexities of Grocery Shopping.................................... 95

Chapter 13
Traditions and Time Management.. 101

Chapter 14
Friend of the Revolution 106

Chapter 15
Small Rebellions 111

Chapter 16
Teaching "Escape English" 118

Chapter 17.. 125

Chapter 18.. 128

Chapter 19
Hunter, Gatherer, Medicine Woman 141

Chapter 20
Wardrobe Malfunctions.. 151

Chapter 21
Orphan Informant 156

Chapter 22
Too Much, Too Soon.. 164

Chapter 23
A Break From the Heartbreak 171

Chapter 24
Not Just Cheese 178

Chapter 25
Alone, but Not Lonely 184

Chapter 26
You've Made a Mistake 192

Chapter 27
Going Back to Cali(fornia) 196

Chapter 28
Closing In 200

Chapter 29
Our American Friends 204

Chapter 30
Playing with Pistachios 207

Chapter 31
Survivor's Guilt 210

Chapter 32
The End of an Era 214

Chapter 33
Oldest Living Friend 219

Epilogue 223

PROLOGUE

On January 3, 2020, then President of the United States – Donald J. Trump – ordered the assassination of Qassem Soleimani, the Iranian General running an elite military wing of Iran's Revolutionary Guards. By January 5, 2020, the stated justification – "imminent threats" – was being challenged. The world was put in the position of holding its breath as the real possibility of yet another costly, prolonged war in the Middle East loomed on the horizon.

In response to the news of Soleimani's death, the streets of Tehran were flooded with millions of mourners, carrying carefully staged photographs of him and chanting *"Marg ba Amrika!"*, Death to America!

The photos of a sea of men, and women draped in black, fists raised with voices in unison, mirror the same scene that played out on our televisions in 1979 following the Iranian Revolution and seizure of the US embassy.

So why do we care? And, more to the point what does this have to do with the experiences of one woman living in a country over forty years ago?

For starters, I have always believed that we should know about a people before we bomb them. I like to think that most people do. I hope.

I also, clearly, have a special interest: I have three handsome Iranian-American sons, men, who I would dearly love to shield from the type of Iranophobic hysterical crap their father faced when we returned from Iran in 1982. I am relatively confident that each of them, intentionally given obvious Fars names, can take care of themselves. But mothers worry.

I went through the horrors of 9/11 and the backlash caused by those Saudi murderers. We, as a nation, have unfortunately started falling prey to the marketing ploy of separating "us" from "them." Painting everyone from a geographical area with the same bias is just plain wrong, and it is something that has plagued our country for years and led to social unrest.

We have home grown terrorists, as do they. They have governments that plot and execute bombing raids and military incursions, and, so do we. And of course, they have clear voices of rational opposition straining to be heard through the beating of the drums of war. Thankfully, so do we.

If we are going to war, we need to be able to distinguish our friends from our enemies. Sometimes, however, our friends have some pretty legitimate beefs. Sadly, the history of US foreign policy in Iran is unflattering.

It has now been over forty years since the Ayatollah stepped off the plane onto Iranian soil. Forty years of conflict and name calling. Forty years of soul crushing economic sanctions, hopeful negotiations resulting in a tenuous nuclear agreement that for one, glorious moment in history actually contributed to world peace.

We, as a nation, made a promise. We then took it away. We broke our promise of peace. We alienated those of our allies that signed on to the deal. We stopped all efforts to loosen economic sanctions that would have helped the average, working Iranian citizen feed her family. We started, again, vilifying an entire nation.

Most people forget that the US and Saddam Hussein were allies, united against the Iranians in the 1980s. Most people forget that the US armed the Taliban to fight against the Soviets in Afghanistan in the 1980s. Ironically, the very General assassinated by a drone in Baghdad on January 3, 2020, worked with other dubious "allies" against ISIS. Politics do, indeed, make strange bedfellows.

Quasam Soleimani was a vile, murderous, maniacally brilliant political opportunist. He ran an elite military wing of the barbaric Revolutionary Guards. He really did not deserve to live. But, before we rush head on into yet another military incursion in Iran and the surrounding countries, we must take a look at the history and lessons that history has—or should have— taught us.

The Iranian people want peace. They do not, however, want to be bullied and insulted and ignored and maligned. As a people, they are fiercely proud of their national heritage and won't shy away from telling anyone who will listen that every single foreign invader from the beginning of time, left Iran with something uniquely Persian to add to their culture. Farsi, the language of Iran, was the official language of the Turkish royal court. The Persian healer, Abu Ali Sina, was the father of modern medicine. The list goes on and on.

And so, when the US government drops a bomb on someone the Iranian regime has turned into a national hero, the people will take to the streets to mourn and yell forty year old slogans. They will rail against the US. They will burn effigies and paint murals. But, they will not hate our people.

Frankly, Iranians have a lot of reason to be angry at the US. In 1953 the Central Intelligence Agency and British government orchestrated a coup that toppled a wildly popular, democratically elected leader and replaced him with a despot. And that was just the start.

I have spent the past forty years of my life displaying an almost evangelical obsession with sharing my "stories" (as my father liked to call them) with anyone with a pulse. After about five minutes of ranting, once I notice my audience has adopted that "deer in the headlights" look, I tend to back off realizing that he or she had really no actual desire to keep up with the current events in a country routinely mispronounced as "eye ran". I would then mercifully volunteer to stop talking. My sudden silence would then invariably prompt them to ask: "So why do they hate us so much?"

And there it was; *that* was my opening.

I have had a unique experience that very, very few women have had that I dare presume may have given me no small amount of insight to share. I want those adventures to start a conversation about our aspirational similarities. I want to put a face on a people; a face that just might belong to my niece or nephew or sister-in-law or friend.

And so, I say again: Should we know about a people before we bomb them?

CHAPTER 1:
UNPLANNED VISITORS

In the fall of 1981, I was at home in Tehran, Iran. The knock on the door surprised me. I was not expecting anyone, let alone three young men in what appeared to be brand-new military uniforms. I opened the door and immediately noticed the AK-47s in their hands. There is nothing quite like the sensation of having fourteen-year-olds pointing loaded automatic rifles at your pregnant belly. They did not smile, nor did they allow their eyes to meet mine. I bowed my head and pulled my scarf down around my face, lowering it to my eyebrows, not daring to make eye contact.

"They've found out about Hadj," my mind screamed. "They know."

"*Saalam, Khanuum,*" grumbled the man who was apparently in charge. "We come in." The formality of *Khanuum*, meaning "missus" or "woman" did little to soften his approach.

They stepped through the doorway and into our cool marble foyer. I stood back, thankful that Hadj, my husband, was not home. I feared that the purpose of this visit was to take him into custody. I prayed he did not decide that today was the day he would come home early.

"*Chaii?*" I asked. "May I bring you tea?"

Without waiting for an answer, I turned away from the men. I walked confidently into the kitchen, my hand cradling my belly. I wanted the men to know I was pregnant, to think of me as a pregnant woman—not a foreigner.

I put the water on to boil and pulled the tray for sweets and tea down from the shelf. On the tray I placed three small tea glasses, each one with a gold rim. I took the concentrated tea from the makeshift samovar that always sat on the stove and poured the dark fluid into each glass. Carefully, I filled the glasses with clear hot water, making sure the tea in each was sufficiently dark. I placed three cubes of raw sugar onto small plates and set the cups next to them. I carried the tray back into the large foyer, where the three men had already made themselves comfortable sitting around the small rectangular table.

"*Beyfarmayeen.*" I gestured. "Please."

The leader looked at the tray, then up at me. His cohorts simply looked at me.

"We must look around now," he said with as much authority as he could muster, refusing the offering.

His hesitant and cautious demeanor strongly suggested to me that I was his first *kharegi* (foreigner). I was certain the other two had never seen a woman of my height or with blue eyes. They all looked suspiciously at my feet. It seemed to amuse them that I was wearing clogs, and now, at over six feet tall, I towered above them.

I bowed my head, placed the tea down on the table, and gestured to it. I did not want to touch it, because as a non-Muslim, I feared this would make my tea *najis* (unclean). I wanted options. I wanted them to look around and go.

"*Beyfarmayeen.*" I gestured again to the tea. "Please have some."

"We don't have time, *Khanuum,*" interrupted the commander, glaring slightly at me. "Let's go," he said, motioning.

They turned from me in unison. My heart skipped a beat as they filed one by one into the small, enclosed kitchen. I had alcohol hidden there. The youngest of the three opened the oven and peered into it. I stood there trying desperately to control my breathing: smiling, smiling, smiling—remembering my mother's admonition to smile in the face of danger and smiled again.

Designed for one servant cook's use, the kitchen was a basic 10x15' room directly off the butler's pantry accessed through a set of double, pane-glass doors. To the left, hidden behind one of these doors, was a portable automatic dishwasher. This Western convenience, purchased by my father-in-law Aghajune for my mother-in-law Iranjune, was so foreign and superfluous to her that it was never used.

One might have thought that it would have been hard to come by alcohol in Iran in 1981 after the Islamic Revolution, but it was not. While alcohol was officially banned, if you had the will and enough money, you could find it. The Armenian Christians made wine and vodka, and our neighbor up the street had access to the best bathtub vodka I'd ever tasted.

"No stems," he would say. "No bad wood alcohol. Pure."

Having a little something on hand that was familiar and forbidden allowed me to feel like a rebel. Discovery of this contraband was a serious offense, however, even for a foreign bride. Hoping that no one would think to look in the unit, I hid my bootleg vodka deep inside the dishwasher. I prayed that my uninvited guests would ignore it too. As I suspected, and to my relief, none of these goons had ever seen an automatic dishwasher before, so they didn't bother to open it up.

Finding nothing of interest in the kitchen, the young men crossed the foyer toward the master bedroom, making a grand show of peering under and around the chairs that lined the walls.

Entering the master bedroom, the leader opened the chest of drawers and gingerly poked around my underwear with the business end of his weapon, as if fearful a snake would suddenly strike. While he entertained himself with my undergarments, his associates took turns peering under the bed and using the butt ends of their weapons to poke around the armoire. They picked up bottles of oils and lotions. They looked in shoeboxes. They ran their hands under the mattress and inspected the perimeters of the carpets. They had a quick look into the bathroom before moving on.

Finishing up with the main house, they trekked out the back door leading to the terraced marble patio that overlooked our garden.

Like most properties in Iran, ours was a walled compound. These walls were erected when the land was first purchased to keep "outsiders" out and to allow people to buy land, hold it for years, and not develop it. The walls clearly delineated property lines and boundaries. The owners would build a small outbuilding on the land and install a caretaker to fend off intruders. It was not uncommon for a family to spend a Saturday having a picnic in their secret garden, using the land as their private getaway.

The wall at the very end of the garden, which ran parallel to the house, backed up against the rear of a neighboring apartment building. The building was attached to the back of our wall and rose above it by two stories. The picture windows of the apartments were darkened but visible from our terrace. We thought a number of members of the Revolutionary Guard (an elite branch of Iran's armed forces) and their families lived in that building, but we weren't sure.

At the base of the wall were a few stray bushes, but it was mainly a patch of dirt. This barren patch was punctuated by the presence of one small but noticeable mound. Buried beneath that mound was a stash of guns and ammunition.

The armories were overrun during the 1979 revolution, causing guns and ammunition to be "liberated" and fall into the hands of civilians. The army, which had turned on the Shah, Iran's pre-revolutionary leader, did little to protect its weaponry. It was said five tanks also went "missing" after the revolution. Rumor had it they were buried somewhere in the great expanse of desert to the south of Tehran.

During the hectic days of the revolution, a bag of guns and ammunition "liberated" from the armory by my brother-in-law appeared at our home and made its way into the dirt that lined the far wall. Hastily created, the mound itself was the unintended result of poor planning. Nevertheless, it had remained there without incident until that day. While the bullets were incompatible with the handguns in the bag, they were still valuable. At the "right time," the bag would have found its use.

As we crossed the terrace overlooking the yard, I became painfully aware of the mound. It seemed to grow in size, pulsating with every beat of my heart. I quickly ushered the trio across the patio, up one step, and into the small studio apartment that stood adjacent to the main house.

I tend to yammer when I am nervous. I try to make small talk. It was, I found, a challenge to engage in small talk in another language with your heart beating into your ears. My mind kept wandering. Would they arrest me? Would I give birth in jail? Would they let me see a doctor? Thank God I didn't really know what Hadj was doing. But would they believe me?

This studio was our residence when Iranjune and Aghajune, were "in residence" in the main house. It was more of a loft than a single-story studio; a lovely "A" design with a flight of stairs leading from the bottom floor to the sleeping area above. When my in-laws made their annual six-month trek to visit their children in Europe and the United States, we moved into their rooms and took over the home. On this day, they were fortuitously en route to Geneva.

I stood smiling, trying not to shake, watching them move through the studio and up to the sleeping loft on the second floor. Apparently, the leader wanted one of the others to watch me, so he positioned an underling near me at the front door.

"Are you Muslim?" my chaperone ventured to ask me.

"I am agnostic," I replied. "The Ayatollah says Jesus was a Prophet too, right? I have not decided."

Being agnostic in Iran at that time was perfectly acceptable. The words for agnosticism are literally "I have not decided." The worst thing I could have done was to try to fake being a Muslim. They would have made me pray, right then and there. My Farsi was conversational by that time, but prayers are memorized in Arabic. I would never have passed.

As I stood there, paralyzed with fear as they continued their search, I realized we had photographs of friends taken during our wedding in California, and I made a mental note to ask Hadj what to do about them. Could the photos pose a risk? Would they link others to us—to him? Were all of the guests still active in "the movement"? Some? A few? I decided then and there to make a sweep of the house and destroy anything that would connect us with any Iranian student-movement types from California.

Immediately to the right of the front door of the studio, on the table near the small kitchenette, sat my precious IBM Selectric typewriter. Only two nights before, I had completed typing an article summing up political events and happenings around the world. Taking articles from every available English-language publication, I would condense them into short blurbs on world events. Once done, just as I had seen in the movies, I would place the articles in an envelope and deposit it at a specific time into a designated trash can in a public park. It was an enormously cloak-and-dagger operation, which required several trips around, through and across the park prior to the drop-off to ensure no one was following me.

Hadj explained to me that these articles then appeared, translated into Farsi, in widely distributed underground, often banned newspapers for people to read. The intention was to broaden peoples' views and offer an analysis of the news from a more socially progressive point of view. In light of the extreme censorship of news coming into the country, we hoped to provide a concentrated summary of an opposing view of world news.

I didn't know who did this or when or how it was done. I only knew that finding papers and publications spread out across that table would have caused the young men in my home to wonder what I was up to. But fate had intervened, and the articles had already left my hands.

The typewriter did, however, cause the leader to give me a questioning look.

"I write letters to my mother," I volunteered. "I tell her about the people of Iran and the revolution," I lied.

"You like our country?" the younger one asked.

"It is my country now. We are *hamvatan*, fellow countrymen. I am Iranian now," I said confidently.

The force of my statement, juxtaposed with my obvious Americanness and bizarre footwear, actually caused them to smile as they left the small apartment and headed back out onto the terrace.

The stairs leading up to the roof hugged the side of the house. One was required, however, to duck under the beam to finish the climb. The roof was bare except for the presence of the small shed housing our swamp cooler, which the group immediately noticed upon reaching the top. Cautiously they approached the structure, and on the order of the leader, one of the men threw open the door of the shed with a dramatic flourish. It was empty, save for the cooler itself.

Disappointed to find nothing on the roof beyond a clear view of the Saad Abad Palace grounds directly across the street from our home, the men turned to descend the stairs and return to the yard. Feeling as if I were home free, I brushed past the group to beat them down the stairs onto the terrace below.

Pushing past his underlings, the leader wanted to be the first of his group to descend the stairs. I watched his face as he slowed his pace, his eyes scanning the yard before him. Suddenly, I saw him pause. The air left my body. I struggled to control my breathing as panic began to set in. His eyes narrowed and I held my breath.

He had noticed the mound.

Rushing to make his way to the stairs, he turned his head slightly, looking down on me as I stood frozen on the landing below. I was, of course, smiling. His eyes fixed on me, he stepped forward and smacked his forehead squarely on the low, metal beam. He hit the beam with such force that it caused him to lose his balance and fall awkwardly backward into the arms of his two cohorts.

His humiliation was stark and apparent. He pulled himself together, rubbing the slowly developing red patch on his forehead with his free hand. His underlings, looking startled, giggled nervously as they tried to avert their eyes from their leader. Turning violently toward them, he hissed a command. The others pulled themselves together and glared at me in unison. I was frozen in place, my smile painted on my face, my eyes blank, my racing heart pounding in my chest.

To this day, the rest is just a blur to me. I recall making a couple of sympathetic sounds, offering ice, doing a little gratuitous fawning and feigning concern. The leader had appeared weak and incompetent in front of me. He had shamed himself. He ignored my offers of assistance just as he ignored the mound, still visible to the naked eye at the end of the garden. It remained undisturbed and thankfully unnoticed.

The men could not get out of my house fast enough.

CHAPTER 2
THE MAKING OF THE RADCLIFFES

I was raised by intellectual gypsy Republicans. My mother and father loved to travel and instilled that love in all of their five children. In 1962 they packed up the family and headed off to Copenhagen, Denmark, for a year. They repeated that exercise in 1967, when we all moved to Troon, Scotland. We traveled for weeks at a time during those days. In 1962 we crammed ourselves into a red-and-white Volkswagen bus, with my youngest brother, Kevin, corralled in his makeshift playpen in the rear. In 1967 we toured in a Peugeot station wagon, using back roads and staying in small family-run inns situated above local pubs. My mother would sit and read aloud from the Michelin Guide. My father routinely wore earplugs.

My parents believed in family above all and fostered in their children a philosophy that family loyalty trumped all other loyalties. They were an unlikely couple: My father was born and raised in California's Imperial Valley, and his family settled in El Centro, a dusty agricultural town not far from the Mexican border. My mother was from a small town in Maine called Turner. While my father's people were distinctly working class, my mother's father owned the local factory that produced sought-after hooked rugs.

My mother and her twin sister were a pair of privileged little girls in matching outfits, their younger brother tagging along behind them. They grew up in a lovely white home near a river, with fields and apple orchards as their playgrounds.

In contrast, my father and his brother lived in a one-bedroom shotgun shack. He and his brother slept on the enclosed porch year-round. His mother was educated, but deaf. Her family had been relatively well-off merchants in Michigan. She had left Mills College for Women in Oakland, California, a few units shy of graduating to marry my grandfather. I always sensed that her family had believed she married beneath her status. But she was disabled, and she thought my grandfather was the best match she could expect. Their life together was no picnic.

When the Great Depression hit, my mother's father lost the factory in Maine. Eleanor Roosevelt, on a regional tour of small businesses during the Depression as First Lady, ordered a large number of oversized rugs from my grandfather's factory. He mortgaged the family home to finance the building of custom-made boxcars in which to transport the rugs. While the rugs were in transit to their final destination, Mrs. Roosevelt canceled the contract. Because of sovereign immunity, citizens cannot sue the government, and so my grandfather lost everything. Years later, after hearing this story, I finally realized why my grandfather always referred to the former first lady as that "goddamn horse-faced woman." She alone had ruined him financially, he felt.

Following the loss of that order, my grandfather disappeared for over two years. Hiding from creditors, he fled from his family too. Now destitute, my mother and her sister were forced to work as live-in servants, known at the time as "hired girls." It remained the most humiliating experience of my mother's life. Proud as she was, the thought of being forced into servitude was more than she could bear. She never forgot those months and the humiliation she felt. It steeled her resolve to never allow herself to be placed in that position again.

Upon graduating from high school, my mother was informed by her father, who had returned home the year before, that he had enrolled her in secretarial school. "Girls do not go to college," he announced over her protests. "It is a waste of good money."

This slight, more than any other single event in my mother's life, shaped her worldview. Her father had limited her. He had told her she could not follow her dreams. She refused to accept this and instilled in each of her children an almost evangelical commitment to living their best lives.

It took many years for my mother to have the opportunity to return to school, but she did so with my father's enthusiastic support upon our return to the United States in 1968. Eventually she graduated from the University of California–Berkeley, a member of the Phi Beta Kappa Society, and obtained her law degree from the University of California–Hastings College of the Law. She practiced law until she passed away at age 85. She, of course, never limited her children, showing support no matter what wild ideas we had. When I drove a meat truck and unloaded eight tons of meat a day, she found it amusing (but not surprising). When my sister, Kim, came to my home to rewire it and lay carpet, my mother's response was, "But of course she did."

My father put himself through two years of junior college at Imperial Valley College and saved just enough money to transfer to UC Berkeley as a junior. No stranger to work, he took odd jobs on campus to finance his education. He worked and studied and eventually joined the navy's Officer's Candidate program when World War II broke out. My father served on the USS. New Mexico from 1944 to 1946, becoming a Lt. Junior Grade USNR Engineer. He was awarded three battle stars for action in the Philippines and off Okinawa. While on leave in uniform in Boston, he met my mother. He charmed her almost immediately, and they married within weeks.

He returned to UC Berkeley to finish his degree with the help of the GI Bill. Originally entering as a chemistry major, my father changed his major to engineering when he returned after the war.

It is not boasting to say that my father, Charles William Radcliffe, was the father of modern prosthetic design. He is the man who designed the component parts of the artificial limbs worn by 99 percent of those needing them in the post–World War II years. He was also the man who convinced the university to obtain one of the first computers on its campus, a computer he used to create designs to assist in helping prosthetists comfortably fit patients with artificial limbs.

He spent his entire professional life teaching in the Department of Mechanical Engineering at UC Berkeley and working with the Veterans Administration and other organizations to properly fit amputees.

His work, the original SACH (solid ankle, cushioned heal) prosthetic foot sits encased in glass at the University of California Medical Center in San Francisco.

I have spent my life bragging about my father. He, however, shunned praise and accolades. He was a simple man who simply loved his children, grandchildren, and great grandchildren. He adored our mother with complete abandon.

And so, these two people from opposite ends of the country and the social spectrum packed their bags and moved to married-student housing in Berkeley, California, eventually moving to the suburbs and raising five children.

CHAPTER 3
UNANTICIPATED COURTSHIP

My parents' story is not uncommon. Many couples met and married swiftly during and after World War II. It was just meant to be. Both believed in hard work. Both believed in independence and self-reliance. They also believed in a strong and loyal family. As their children, we were raised to follow our passions, define our dreams and, most of all, live full and complete lives. My parents taught these values to my brothers, my sister, and me.

In 1978 it was not a huge surprise, therefore, when I announced to my parents that I would be traveling alone, halfway around the world to Iran, a country in the midst of political chaos.

But my penchant for travel had revealed itself before, in 1972, during my first year at UC Berkeley. At 18 years old, I came home from college one day and announced I would be studying in France for a year. I found my mother sitting, as she often did, at the kitchen table, torts textbook open, coffee cup full, a cigarette smoldering in a nearby ashtray, and I simply informed her I would be leaving the following winter.

"Well, that's nice, honey," she said, not looking up. "You realize your father and I can't pay for this, right?"

"I know. I never expected you to. I'll make my own money," I replied, almost defiantly.

I scooped ice cream at a shop on Durant Avenue in Berkeley. I painted the basement of a home in Oakland while simultaneously landscaping the yard and watching the homeowners' four children. I cleaned houses. I did anything I could to make a buck. After months of labor, I was able to amass enough money to purchase my airfare to Paris and a third-class EuroRail pass, with a little left over for living. My plan was not actually fully hatched, and my budget was slim. I would fly with my friend to Paris on New Year's Eve 1973.

I wish I could say that my time in France was wholly productive, but it really was not. I ended up staying with a blended family composed of eleven children from two former marriages, living in a huge home in the suburbs north of Paris. I later moved to the coastal town of Deauville, in Normandy, where I lived with the Parisian family's adult daughter and her boyfriend. While in Deauville, I worked under the table at Le Pony Club, renting out horses by day and serving beer at night.

I was an anomaly in Deauville. The city had a small permanent population in the off-season that would increase exponentially during the tourist season, when its casinos, racetracks, and film festivals attracted the rich and famous. I was the resident *jeune fille américaine* (the American girl). I had no real friends but many acquaintances. I felt no connection to anyone in particular and spent a great deal of time drinking to while away the hours. This made me the object of gossip and disdain for reasons I didn't understand at the time. Women would attack me in clubs because they thought I had designs on their boyfriends. I did not. I was just trying to find my place.

After months of feeling aimless, I woke up one morning in late summer 1975, clear that it was time to leave. I fished my return airplane ticket out from the bottom of my suitcase, packed my things, wrote a thank-you note to my host family, and left town. As I flew back to California, I still had no idea what I wanted to do. I had not yet found my passion. I assumed that I was expected to finish college, although I couldn't decide on a major. I ended up taking the easy route, declaring myself a French literature major. I was apathetic but searching, passive but seeking passion. I was, in a word, lost.

One afternoon, shortly after my return to the United States and unable to move back into the dormitory and needing a place to live, I showed up at a women's boarding house on College Avenue in Berkeley. Those were the days when the university allowed students to take a leave of absence, then return and reenroll. I was scheduled to return to school in the fall of 1975.

The boarding house was a neat, two-story structure with lime-green shag carpeting throughout the common areas. It was a classic Victorian, with a large formal living room, a dining room of substantial size, and a good-sized functional kitchen. The second floor held four big bedrooms and a full bath; the ample basement had two additional unpermitted and possibly illegal rooms and another bathroom. Eighteen women lived in that house. Eighteen women shared one refrigerator.

Directly behind the kitchen was a full bathroom. Next to the bathroom was a roomy pantry with a window. The pantry had no closets but was wide enough for a twin bed and a chest of drawers. I talked the landlord into letting me rent the pantry for $75 a month. All that and a private bath—I was in renter's heaven!

It was in that house that I met Hadj for the first time. I had no way of knowing the impact that chance meeting would have on me and the path my life would take from that point forward.

. . .

I did not suddenly become a "revolutionary." I was slowly and cautiously introduced to these new ideals by Hadj, whose ability to persuade was the stuff of legend. I realize now that this gradual but systematic approach to politics was his version of seduction. I had seen the gilded palaces of Europe and the slums that often stood a few blocks away. I had written a letter to Nixon imploring him to address the housing inequalities I saw featured in Life magazine.

Over my brief lifetime, I had developed a keen awareness of social injustice as my family never shied away from discussing such topics around our dinner table. But it was Hadj who released in me a real passion for social change and activism.

Hadj was fifteen years older than me and had lived through the exciting and turbulent times of the 1960s, marching the streets with antiwar protesters across the United States, facing water cannons and jail time for his efforts. He spent a week five stories below ground in the infamous New York City jail known as "The Tombs." He was kept awake by glaring overhead lights, and the guards would periodically "clean" the cells by shooting water from hoses through the bars. Undaunted and with great idealism, Hadj continued to fight the fight because he felt it was always the right thing to do.

Hadj's world revolved around politics and political activism. He embraced the structure that was the then-current Maoist thought with enormous vigor. He loved routine and order: His shirts hung in the closet one inch apart. He attempted to ration squares of toilet paper. He served tea with a single cookie neatly placed on the side of the saucer. He made me the same thing for lunch every single day.

But I am burying the lede. The real point here is that after we married, he made me lunch *every single day* without complaint or criticism. His routine was how he expressed love, and I, then too childish to fully grasp this, reveled in annoying him by disrupting his routine any chance I could get.

We met on a Saturday afternoon in the fall of 1975. I was sitting at the long communal dining table in the women's boarding house on College Avenue, wearing a wholly unattractive head scarf to camouflage the fact that I needed to wash my hair, when Hadj sat down facing me.

"What do you think of the situation in the Middle East?" he asked, without bothering to introduce himself.

"I don't think of the situation in the Middle East," I replied, somewhat annoyed.

"You should," he stated emphatically.

"Thanks for the suggestion." I responded, dismissively.

My first impression of Hadj was that he was too intense and too good-looking. He was over six feet, which is tall for an Iranian. When I first met him, he had a shock of graying, curly hair in a carefully unkempt Afro. Later, he would go to his old girlfriend, and she would cut it shorter, closer to the head, but still long enough to be wavy and distinguished. I used to tell people that Hadj looked the way the actor Omar Sharif wanted to look.

Hadj had immigrated to the United States in 1959 as an eager college student. He enrolled in a small liberal arts school in Minnesota, where he was, he would say, the only person with black hair for fifty miles around. When he first arrived, he was young, handsome, and not particularly interested in politics. He wore tight black suits, as was the fashion, and drove a black Cadillac convertible around town. He was quite the ladies' man. He found himself, however, in a country where opinions were openly expressed and dissent was tolerated. While Minnesota was not a hotbed of radical activity, the collegiate environment coupled with open access to information led Hadj to further question what was going on in Iran at the time.

As a teenager, Hadj had been greatly influenced by the rise of Mohammad Mossadegh, a popular nationalist politician famous for his obstinate refusal to compromise on his principles and for his overwhelming love of country. In 1951, Mossadegh was democratically elected to be Iran's new prime minister. At the time, the then Anglo-Iranian Oil Company—now British Petroleum (BP)—controlled Iran's vast oil reserves. Under the arrangement of the time, the Iranian government actually earned less in revenue from its own oil than the Anglo-Iranian Oil Company paid out to the British in taxes. In short, the Iranian government lost money for each barrel of oil produced and sold.

Within one month of his election, Mossadegh nationalized Iranian oil—to the horror of the British. The United States, which had initially failed to take a strong position, eventually sided with the British. Within two years, in 1953, the US Central Intelligence Agency (CIA) engineered a coup and removed Mossadegh from power. He lived out the rest of his life under house arrest.

With Mossadegh deposed, power in Iran was transferred to the sitting monarch, Mohammad Reza Pahlavi, the Shah (or King) of Iran. Pahlavi had fled Iran as the coup unfolded but returned triumphantly after Mossadegh was toppled. He ruled as "the Shah" and while he liberalized and modernized many aspects of Iranian society, he ruled as an autocrat and political opponents suffered enormously.

Like most despots, maintaining power meant maintaining control. The Shah's secret police, the Organization of National Security and Information, known as the SAVAK, were brutal, feared, and seemingly omnipresent in Iranian society. Their reach extended far beyond Iran's borders, and they routinely sent agents to monitor the activities of Iranians outside of Iran.

After suffering through his first winter in Minnesota, and with a nascent political sensibility, Hadj transferred to the California Polytechnic State University (Cal Poly) located in the coastal town of San Luis Obispo. It was at Cal Poly in 1960 that Hadj and a couple of other newly politicized Iranian students formed what would later become a powerful part of the then-nascent Iranian Students Association (ISA).

The ISA was originally an organization founded and supported by the Iranian and US governments in 1954 as a purported student organization. It was not an organization of activists and was even funded, in part, by the United States Agency for International Development (USAID).

In 1960, however, a new anti-Shah student movement began to rise, which gave birth to the ISA formed by Hadj and his cohorts. To distinguish themselves clearly from the government funded organization, ISA became a part of the Confederation of Iranian Students (National Union).

The newly formed ISA was an organization comprised of chapters located on college, university, and community college campuses across the United States. It was a secular group that dedicated itself to forming a democratic Iran by organizing programs to draw attention to the political situation in that country. It sponsored seminars and meetings. It held cultural nights, inviting representatives of other international organizations to share songs and dances. It organized protest demonstrations with coalitions of other groups, churches, and clubs to inform the American people about US financial and political support for the dictatorship of the Shah of Iran.

From its inception and over the next two decades, the ISA grew to be an international organization with tens of thousands of active supporters. Its members were the students seen on television in the late 1970s protesting against the Shah's regime, wearing paper bags over their heads to protect their identities. Being a vocal supporter of the group outside of Iran could subject their family members to terrifying interrogations in Iran by the secret police. Leaders, such as Hadj, could not return to Iran, under threat of imprisonment and summary execution.

The ISA was a democratic organization with leftist leanings, open to any Iranian student with a desire to work towards a democratic, secular Iran. The leadership of the ISA was broken into various "secretariats," or areas of responsibility. There were cultural secretariats, who oversaw plays and presentations and cultural events, and political secretariats, who developed political theory and platforms for the organization. Hadj was *always* voted in as the international relations secretary, charged with bringing together coalitions of different groups to support the cause. His ability to motivate people, his enormous personal charm, and his knowledge of international affairs made him perfectly suited to this task. He met with progressives of all flavors. He ate lamb and bread with Palestinians. He communed with the progressive Christians and charmed the Filipinos. He pulled coalitions together, causing incredibly diverse organizations and individuals to work as one for a single cause—his single cause: a free Iran. He was a force of nature and a force that could rarely be resisted.

When Hadj and I first met, the US immigration authorities were attempting to deport him. Apparently, at that time, student activists were not particularly welcome in the United States, especially ones who had overstayed their visas, as Hadj had done. Hadj could not, however, return to Iran. The notorious Iranian secret police organization, SAVAK, had a death warrant out on him. SAVAK was known for its history of brutally imprisoning and torturing dissident voices in Iran, and would not have hesitated to execute Hadj had he been forced to return to Iran. As a result, Hadj was seeking political asylum. The US immigration authorities, however, were not eager to grant it. To concede that an outspoken critic of the Shah would face certain death if deported would acknowledge to the world that an ally of the United States engaged in human-rights violations. As one might recall, in December 1977, US president Jimmy Carter traveled to Iran and toasted the Shah by declaring Iran to be an "island of tranquility in a sea of unrest."

Allowing Hadj to remain in the United States also would have created a precedent for other Iranian students. Therefore, the Immigration and Naturalization Service (INS) as the Department of Homeland Security was then called, was not going to make it easy for Hadj to assert the danger he was in. Every time he would attempt to enter evidence of Iranian torture, the authorities would object to it as irrelevant. The politics of our then-ally could not be brought into the arena and Hadj had to demonstrate, very specifically, the direct danger he faced. It was an uphill battle with serious consequences.

Thankfully our marriage ended the entire nightmare. The INS was understandably suspicious of our marriage, which took place in the middle of the deportation hearings. The organization believed initially that it was a fake marriage. We suffered through interview after interview: What color are your bedsheets? What is the color of your husband's favorite sweater? How many towels do you have in your bathroom? Finally, after interviewing us, our immediate neighbors (all of whom were foreign students, terrified by the knock on their doors by the INS!), and our landlady, the government granted Hadj permanent residency and a green card.

* * *

Ours was not a particularly romantic courtship. One day, only a few months into our relationship, Hadj summoned me to meet him at the International House in Berkeley. The International House was not a pancake restaurant. It was a residence and meeting hall dedicated to housing foreign students at UC Berkeley. Aside from the rooms, it had one of the better coffee shops in town.

Thinking that Hadj had some leaflet for me to edit or a meeting for me to attend, I dutifully walked down College Avenue and turned uphill onto Bancroft to trek to the International House coffee shop. When I arrived, Hadj was already seated at a table, looking even more intense than usual. I grabbed a coffee and joined him.

"Lisa*Khanuum*," he started, "I have decided that we will spend the rest of our lives together."

"Oh, you have?" I replied, slightly annoyed by the presumptuousness of that statement. "And why is that?"

"You come from a good family. We will get married. But," he hesitated, leaning in toward me even more intensely, "you *must* learn about my language and my culture. I cannot go to Iran, but you can. You will go."

And so there it was—his "proposal." He did not drop to one knee. There were no expressions of undying love and devotion. It was simple and straightforward. He had a plan. He had decided I was the one. I, for my part, young and up for an adventure figured "why the hell not?"

We were married at my parents' house in January 1977, in a small ceremony presided over by a judge my mother knew. I had no desire for a big, elaborate affair and paid a friend of mine who was desperate for money fifty dollars to make me a simple wedding dress of unbleached muslin.

Only about twenty or so of our closest friends attended. They were occasional drinkers. I, however, come from a loud, talkative family of big drinkers. My parents had ordered two bottles of champagne per guest.

"I don't want to run out of champagne and ruin the party," my dad declared matter-of-factly.

Our wedding was great fun, and our Iranian friends suffered for it. Days later they would call, moaning into the phone about their hangovers and confessing that they thought the champagne was more like 7Up than alcohol. The morning after the wedding, I left our Berkeley apartment to head out to San Francisco to protest the closure of a transient hotel in Chinatown. Hadj went to meetings. That was "us" in a nutshell.

I was young, and marrying Hadj seemed like a great adventure. I was completely besotted by him, of course. I was easygoing and up for any adventure. I trusted him completely and knew he would look out for me. He had an ever-present aura of personal power that I found compelling and comforting. He was a respected leader and I loved basking in his reflective glory. Moreover, I allowed him to think he could boss me around, which I found amusing. Sure, I would learn the language. Sure, I would travel. Sure, I would spend the rest of my life with him. Sure. Hadj was not a poet. He was a natural-born charismatic leader who spoke in short, declarative sentences, and gave commands. He was thirty-seven and I was not yet twenty-three.

During those early days of our marriage he supported himself as a waiter in expensive and exclusive restaurants. He hated being forced to wear a tuxedo, to bow and scrape, but he loved the tips. He was exceedingly popular with the female clientele. He would come home at night, laughing as he emptied his pockets of slips of paper or matchbooks containing the phone numbers of some hopeful women.

"Lisa*Khanuum*, see? I am very popular," he would say.

Despite the constant and often aggressive attentions of other women, Hadj would have rather shoved hot pokers in his eyes before cheating on me. He was just that kind of man. Loyalty was everything. There was never a single moment, during the entire length of our marriage, when I doubted that Hadj would jump in front of a moving train for me. Never.

Every Saturday morning, without exception, we would do the laundry and clean our apartment. While I folded or hung his shirts (often just stuffing mine in a drawer), Hadj would (to the absolute delight of our elderly landlady, who lived across from us), take it upon himself to sweep the common area and driveway of our small complex. It was our routine and I would regularly have a minor tantrum about it. I chafed at the control Hadj felt he needed to maintain. I believe I actually found myself saying out loud, with a straight face, "You're not the boss of me" on many occasions. Oh, to be that young again!

On Sundays we would drive to Fort Cronkhite on the northern, Marin County, side of the Golden Gate Bridge, assuming we had no demonstration in which to march or political meeting to attend. Taking the freeway from Berkeley across the Bay Bridge, we would stop to wander San Francisco's North Beach neighborhood. Hadj would regale me with stories of marches or passing out leaflets in the nearby public housing projects or meetings with union representatives and clergy.

The first time we made this trip to Fort Cronkhite while dating and during the "be a good sport" period that some women go through for a man, Hadj assured me that at the very top of the steep hill that tumbled from the sky to the cliffs over Rodeo Beach below was an "officer's club" stocked with coffee and soda.

"Officer's club? Really?" I complained.

"It's just a little higher," he promised. "Just right here, a little more."

Red-faced and panting, I trudged up that damn hill in search of coffee. But there was no officer's club. There was no coffee. There was only a concrete platform jutting out from the remains of a WWII abandoned bunker. I was furious, but the view was spectacular. I vowed never to be taken in by Hadj again. It was a vow broken so many times I have lost count. He was a charmer.

The Sunday routine to Fort Cronkhite lasted until we departed for Iran and recommenced upon our return. Each son later born to us was carted up those hills, some complaining as I had and some not, and all having been told the story of mommy and the officer's club. Hadj would recall his deceit with tears forming in his eyes and his head thrown back with the full force of his laughter.

It was in early 1978 that Hadj informed me that I would be going to Iran to attend his brother's wedding. Regular protests had begun in Iran, fostered and encouraged by Komeini and other significant religious leaders. With each protest, students and dissidents were murdered by the Shah's forces. In Iran, the period of mourning is 40 days. And so, in 40-day intervals, demonstrators would hit the streets in protest.

"Lisa*khanuum*"," he declared one evening after dinner, "My brother is marrying some woman. I want you to go to represent me. I cannot go, of course. I want you to learn as much about the political situation as possible." His delivery was curt and emphatic.

"You must be my eyes and ears," he instructed. "You must listen and watch and be very, very careful what you say," he cautioned.

"I have not been back for a long time. I have not seen most of my relatives, except only my immediate family, for decades," he informed me. "In this atmosphere, you have no idea who you can trust."

Half listening to his instructions, I started to plan my adventure in my head. I was thrilled by the prospect of adventure and terrified at the same time. However, I am ashamed to admit that my thoughts did not immediately go to political recon, but rather what I should pack for the occasion.

"What should I wear?" I asked Hadj somewhat sheepishly.

"A long dress," he replied.

CHAPTER 4
HOMECOMING

It was a smoldering-hot day in April 1978 when I arrived in Iran at Tehran International Airport. I was terrified, holding my breath as we descended through the smoggy haze that shrouded the city. Knowing the regime had a death warrant out for my husband didn't help matters, and I feared his reputation and standing as *persona non grata* would put me in jeopardy. I had planned on staying until early fall, collecting as much information about the growing rebellion as I could. As the plane descended, visions of months spent in a small cell, torture, and abuse filled my thoughts. Was I strong enough to resist? Doubtful, I instinctively thought. I am a chickenshit coward beneath lots of bravado. At the first sign of cattle prods, I'd spew.

Iran in 1978 was not a place Hadj could be. The Shah and his government wanted him dead for his role in organizing student opposition. They wanted the student movement that he started dead. They wanted a lot of things dead. I was sent to Iran in his stead—my mission was to attend a wedding, check out the situation, learn as much about the political atmosphere as I could, and report back. My heart was beating out of my chest.

The captain announced our final descent into the airport. As I looked out of the window, all I could see was an expanse of gray—gray skies, gray buildings, gray dust blowing in the heat. Tehran, not unlike Los Angeles, sits in a basin, with a crown formed by the Elburz Mountains to the north. The Elburz range, in tandem with the basin, tends to corral the smog so that it hangs like a shroud over the entire city.

We circled Tehran, landed without incident, and taxied to the terminal. As the doors opened and the stairs were unceremoniously pushed outward against the side of the plane, my breath quickened. I began to sing to myself—it's what I do when I'm nervous. Then I entered the blast furnace that was Tehran.

The smell of diesel fuel mixed with sweat hit me as we were herded into the waiting buses on the tarmac. I stood there, silently bracing myself as the bus sped to the terminal and came to an abrupt stop. Passport in hand, I placed myself in line, ready to confront the border agent who would process my entry.

This was not my first rodeo. I'd had some prior experience with hostile border guards. Years before, when my parents had taken all five of us kids in a VW bus across Europe, some cranky Spanish border guards gave us grief as we attempted to cross into France. My dad, being an expert in the design and fitting of artificial legs, had placed a crate of disassembled artificial limbs in the van. They were packed carefully underneath the mattress that covered the entire rear of the bus—a makeshift crib to keep my baby brother, Kevin, happy.

To our dismay the guards were pretty sure my father was attempting to smuggle nuclear weapons into their country. Our van was emptied of all passengers and contents, seats, hubcaps, every-thing. Suitcases were unceremoniously opened and clothing tossed. My father was taken into a small, hot room, where he tried to explain the crate of mysterious polished aluminum parts with his high-school Spanish.

My mother—trooper that she was—turned the event into an adventure. She dedicated herself to making the best of what was a terrifying, tense situation. It was important to her that none of us felt fear. I was seven and the youngest girl. My baby brother was less than two. My other siblings, Bill, Kim, and Clark, were older than I and thoughtfully spaced in two-year intervals.

"Just smile," she chirped. "Let's be friendly and it'll all be fine and dandy."

Her words have remained with me to this day. On that hot, gray, terrifying day in the spring of 1978, they were particularly helpful.

"Passport," mumbled the uniformed customs agent with a slightly bored, clearly disdainful look. "Please give it to me," he added with a perfunctory nod.

"I am here for a wedding," I volunteered a little too quickly.

Big grin.

The border guard opened the passport to my photo and looked up briefly to compare it to me (smile, nod). Still holding it open, he began to compare it to a list of what I could only presume were names written in Farsi. He used the index finger of his right hand to run down the list. I watched, smiling inanely, his finger moving quickly down the page until it came to a stop at a place with writing marked conspicuously with a bright red dot. He stopped and looked at me coldly. I froze. I smiled. Time stood still. It must be Hadj's family name, I thought as the air left my body. This is it. They will arrest me now. I will rot in an Iranian jail.

"What is the purpose of your visit?" he asked, slowly, in English.

Controlling the urge to over share, I simply repeated, "I am here for a wedding." Another huge smile.

He nodded and once again opened my passport, inspecting it. With great flourish, he placed the document on top of his small, raised desk. Then he stamped it. I was in, I thought. Did I dodge a bullet? I wondered. It didn't matter. I was there. I was in Iran.

Breathing heavily, I walked toward baggage claim and spotted a familiar face. It was my father-in-law, Aghajune. I recognized him instantly: handsome, graceful, and elegant, an older version of my husband. He was also exceedingly nervous about my being there. He was nearly five feet nine inches tall, with a mass of white hair combed straight back off his forehead. Like his son, he sported a mustache and a wicked grin when he wanted to. His eyes were full, black, and soulful. When the time was right, he was wont to burst into song for no apparent reason.

Aghajune was my father-in-law's nickname, a name of endearment used by his family. (*Agha* means "mister." *June* means "dear." I was known as *Lisajune*. My husband called me Lisa*Khanuum*, the *khanuum* part meaning "woman" or "lady" or "missus," depending on the circumstance.) Standing next to Aghajune was a tall, thin young man about my age. I recognized him as well. He was my nephew by marriage, Sayed.

After the appropriate greetings, we grabbed my bags and I was placed into the back of a waiting Mercedes. The sun had gone down and the fading light shone through the grayness and heat. I breathed a sigh of relief, relaxed slightly, settled into the backseat, and stared out the window.

Sayed had visited the United States and spoke excellent English. He was excited about my being in Iran, excited about the prospect of a revolution, and he chatted pleasantly about the sights as we drove from the airport. He was studying medicine at Tehran University. He has since become a respected doctor and teacher, and he is married, with four children of his own.

In 1978 Tehran was a big city of gray buildings and open trench gutters. The main boulevard ran north to south and was lined by mulberry trees that offered delicate shade. In the north end of the city, where the wealthier citizens lived, the streets leading from the main boulevard had trees shading the sidewalks. By and large, the smaller streets, or *ku chehs*, were simply narrow roadways sandwiched between the fronts of buildings and walled courtyards. Often, in the poorer areas, people would use the canals as if they were streams, washing and cleaning clothes in the murky water.

In the northern neighborhoods like Tadjrich, the wealthier part of the city, the open trenches were covered and replaced with pipes buried under the streets. Often, however, during the winter snows, the underground pipes would be unable to contain the melting snows, and sheets of ice would lurk dangerously disguised by a thin layer of dirt and grime near the edge of the sidewalk. North Tehran was at an elevation of approximately 3,500 feet. South Tehran was much closer to sea level. The net effect meant the winter months brought four to five feet of snow in the north and rains in the south.

In the summer heat, the city often smelled of diesel mixed with rotting vegetables—the result of households dumping their collective trash in the open sewers or vacant lots, to be washed away with the rains. Inadvertent dams of old plastic bags would collect in the sewer trenches, causing the waters to overflow from time to time. Home – and business-owners with driveways engineered small paved bridges over the sidewalk from the street wide enough to allow a car or truck to pass over.

Turning off the freeway onto the main boulevard, we began to slowly weave our way through the traffic heading north to the Tajrish neighborhood. Aghajune, ever a conservative driver, drove slower than the rest and somewhat more cautiously. He spoke only a few words of English and my Farsi was even more limited. He fancied himself a French-speaker, and we attempted to communicate until it became too painfully difficult.

"*C'est jolie? Non?*" he asked.

"*Oui, c'est jolie,*" I lied. It was not pretty. It was strange and scary.

I sat back searching the scenery for something, anything familiar. Everything looked so truly foreign to me. It reminded me a little of Mexico, with the strings of lights. It reminded me a little of Rome, with the undisciplined traffic. I was exhausted from my six-hour flight from London but exhilarated at being there at last.

"Can I do this?" I questioned.

"For once in your life keep your mouth shut and your ears open," my mind screamed. My racing heart pumping and adrenaline rushing, I took deep breathes to calm my nerves. I knew I was there to learn and observe, but my pretext was the wedding party. I would be on display as the American Bride of the eldest son, brother of the groom. Hadj's reputation and status in the student movement was known to all and I assumed they would be curious about me.

"Shit!" I caught myself hissing under my breath, "what have I gotten myself into?"

CHAPTER 5
GETTING ACQUAINTED

My grandma used to say, "If I knew you were comin', I'd a baked a cake."

In Iran, it's a tad different. When they know you are coming, they will kill a sheep—really.

Our car turned left up an artery offshoot of the main boulevard, heading uphill into a residential neighborhood. We were close to home, I suspected.

"When we get to the house," my nephew Sayed cautioned, "they want to do something, ah, different."

"Do what?" I asked.

"Well, they want to honor you, you know."

"Really? How?"

"We have a tradition," he started. "When someone comes home after a long journey, we kill a sheep and give some of the meat to the poor."

"Well, how nice," I replied, secretly appalled.

"Yes, it is nice," he agreed, "but we do it in front of you."

"You kill the sheep *in front* of me?" I asked, horrified. "I mean, like, while I am just standing there?"

"Ah…well…yes," he said. "When you get out of the car, they will do it."

"Great. Just great," I thought.

Our car made its final left turn. At the bend in the road I could see the gates of Saad Abad Palace. Saad Abad Palace was built in the 19th century and was home to the Shah's father, Reza Shah in the 1920s. Prior to the revolution in 1979, it was also the then-reigning Shah's residence and remained so until after the revolution when it was turned into a museum.

The guards stood, leaning up against the pillars on either side of the ornate palace gates, rifles slung casually over their shoulders. As our car approached, they appeared to take note. We made eye contact. I smiled. Again.

We drove up to the house, crossing into the oncoming lane to park directly in front of the metal door. The home, a modern one-story brick house, sat level on the slope of the street so that the down-hill end of the home appeared to be taller than the uphill end.

As the car approached I frantically searched for the animal sacrifice. No woolly victim was in sight. I let out an audible sigh of relief.

"I guess they did not want to scare you," Sayed announced, sensing my relief.

"Yeah. Great. No sheep." I would later be told that, indeed, an animal had been slaughtered and the meat had been distributed to the poor in my honor. I really would have preferred the cake.

As I stepped from the car, my husband's family—his mother and sisters and their children—crowded around me. We kissed each other's cheeks and exchanged greetings. I nodded and smiled. It was overwhelming. An elderly lady swung a brass incense holder around and around in circles, filling the air with acrid smoke. This was, apparently, another welcoming gesture. I was completely unprepared for any of it.

"Thanks, Hadj, for the heads-up," I thought. "Way to prepare me!"

We entered the home and stood staring at each other in the large, open foyer. Iranjune, my mother-in-law, motioned me to come and sit in the formal lounge. Hot, dark tea was served in small glasses. Rosewater-flavored cookies appeared. Sisters-in-law fussed and fretted. Pleasantries were exchanged until I finally fell into bed that night, exhausted.

I woke my first morning to sunlight flooding the room and wondered what the day would hold for me. It was perhaps ten o'clock in the morning, and the household had been up for hours. My mother-in-law, who awoke at sunrise to pray each morning, was busying herself in the kitchen. My father-in-law was sitting at an informal table in the foyer, reading some papers. An elderly manservant called *Baba*, which is actually slang for "daddy," was moving slowly around the house, theoretically pushing a broom. My brother-in-law Hossein, the groom, who still occupied the apartment attached to the house pending his upcoming wedding, had left earlier that morning to work..

As I ventured into the kitchen, my mother-in-law Iranjune ran out to greet me. She was a tiny, wonderful woman barely five feet tall, with smiling eyes and a warm demeanor. When she laughed, like

Hadj, her eyes would sparkle and tears would well up until she could take it no longer and burst into a howl of delight.

She had a mass of auburn hair that fell back from her face onto her shoulders. She wore a black skirt that hit her below the knees and an apron over her casual blouse. She was a ball of energy—cutting, cleaning, making, and doing. I loved her the first minute I saw her and continued to love her until the day she died.

"Lisajune, how are you? *Bia Bisheen, sohbhaneh bohkor.*" (Come, sit, eat breakfast). She motioned vigorously for me to sit at the table in the foyer with Aghajune, and rushed into the kitchen.

"Iranjune," I said towering over her in the small kitchen. "*Man mehmoon nistam* (I am not a guest)," I declared emphatically, using up almost the entire extent of my vocabulary.

"Thank you very much, Lisajune. Here, eat," she replied.

She pointed to the tray sitting on the countertop. A small plate containing feta cheese and herbs sat atop several pieces of warm, soft flatbread. A glass of tea completed the scene—my first breakfast in Tehran.

Iranjune had married Aghajune when she was barely 14 years old, common in Iran. Family was the most important thing to her. She would surround herself with her children, all sitting on or near her like puppies on the sofa, and would laugh until she wept. Her deep, brown, almond-shaped eyes can be seen on my eldest son, warm and full of expression and compassion.

During all the years I knew her, she was always studying to learn English. She would routinely start a sentence with "Thank you very much," which I found endearing and never corrected. Years later, when Hadj's parents moved to California, Iranjune spent months studying for the driver's license test. Her greatest desire was to attain independence by driving her very own car. She got the car, but was never able to pass that test. It did not deter her; she kept on trying year after year, month after month, until her death.

"I read when I pray," she told me one day, while sifting through lentils in search of stones. "I think Aghajune didn't want me to learn to read, but I did," she said haltingly. "When I get up after I pray, I read."

Kneeling on her prayer rug, Iranjune would cover herself with a pale-blue chador, bending forward, reciting the Arabic verse of Islamic prayer. Still covered with that chador and in her own small act of defiance, she stayed each day to struggle with another chapter in her English lesson book. I suspect that time alone, undisturbed by the demands of children and spouse, was precious to her.

* * *

The Ayatollah Khomeini came from a distinguished family whose origins traced back to the daughter of the Prophet Mohammad, Fatimeh. He spent his early years as distinguished member of the clergy in the holy city of Qom, Iran. Over the years, and following the 1953 Coup d'etat, Khomeini's political influence began to grow and mature. By 1964 he was compelled to leave the country, moving initially to Turkey but ending up finally in Najaf, Iraq, a city located near the southwestern border of Iran.

Although exiled from the country, Khomeini continued to develop his theory of an Iranian Islamic Revolution. Publishing works and producing speeches, his words were smuggled into Iran and passed from student to student, follower to follower, for over a decade. Khomeini declared that Islam "is the religion of militant individuals who are committed to truth and justice." In the face of increasing political repression by the Shah, growing distrust of "western values," these words clearly resonated with Iran's young and disaffected.

Our nephew Sayed was a follower and a believer. On one of the many sunny days following my arrival we drove around the city in a tiny Renault 5, weaving in and out of the choking traffic, with Sayed periodically pointing out the sights and discussing the politics. I sat back listening and soaking up the sights and smells, white-knuckling it as he darted deftly between cars and missed fearless pedestrians.

Anti-regime graffiti had begun to show up on walls and buildings throughout the city. Soldiers and police had started to congregate in the various large traffic circles or *meydoons*. Positioned with guns prominently displayed, leaning casually against walls or trees, they waited and watched, ever vigilant of the mass of pedestrians crowding the sidewalks to make sure no crowds congregated. Larger forces were stationed in front of what I could only surmise at the time were important government buildings or offices.

Rumors spread fast in Tehran. It was a big city with a small-town feel. One day I would be told that Americans should keep off the streets; on another day I would be told to avoid a certain section of town. On days like this, foreigners were advised to exercise a little restraint and stay home. My nephew would come over on those mornings and suggest that I just hang out around the house. It was evident that he was excited about the prospect of more demonstrations—more actions to weaken and isolate the Shah.

Emotions ran high during those early days of 1978. People had had enough. In early January, students organized strikes and protest marches. They were joined by thousands of other supporters. Troops had opened fire on protesters—killing dozens. As is the Islamic tradition of mourning and remembrance, 40 days following the killings further demonstrations occurred. This 40-day pattern of mass protest, police killings and responsive protests 40 days later, continued throughout all of 1978.

On the safe days, my nephew and I drove the streets as if our physical presence outside, among the masses, would make us closer to the action. We respected each other. I was the first American he had hosted in his own country. He had visited California briefly and had found himself more of an observer than a fan. He was going through a lot of changes. He was slowly and profoundly being influenced by Khomeini's tapes.

Fortunately, he was more impressed with me than he was with most of the other American visitors he saw around town from time to time.

I will never forget one hot and dusty afternoon when we were driving on a potholed freeway. As we moved through the traffic, I spied what was clearly a young American woman, walking while wearing cut-offs and an American logo'd T-shirt. Sayed saw her too. It was a strange sight: a lone teenager, walking carelessly along the side of a freeway, arms swinging at her side. Apparently, no one had told her to stay inside or conform to local customs. My nephew was furious.

"See!" he shouted over the roar of the open window. "Look at her. No Iranian girl would dress like that. This is what I have been talking about," he declared, gesturing wildly towards the girl.

"They think because they are American, they can do whatever they want."

We sat in silence as he drove. Returning home, Sayed continued to dwell on the sight of the young western woman we had just seen.

"The Shah wanted us all to become westernized," Sayed declared as he draped himself across the arm of the large, red velvet sofa placed prominently in our massive living room. Long and thin, his legs almost reached the floor as he reclined comfortably.

"We want to have our own values," he continued. "Western values conflict with Isalm's values. Period."

I found this statement almost ironic. Here we sat in a large, western home on large western furniture, a large western woman and a modern, English speaking Iranian man of almost my age, making broad, wholesale statements trashing "westernization."

"Really?" I challenged. "You think that people are protesting because they don't want to be westernized? That's insane."

"What about the political repression? What about the total lack of freedom of speech? Thought? Assembly? The damned press."

The word press hissed out of my mouth as I now stood, hands on hips, almost defiantly challenging him. He swung his long legs around to the floor, drawing himself up he matched my posturing.

"You really think Islam is going to liberate your people? How?" I demanded. "You tell me exactly how you think a religion is going to make people here more free."

I realized then that to my American thinking Iran needed an American-type Constitution with all of its stated protections of speech and thought, and, assembly. In my head, Iran's revolution had to mirror America's revolution both in form and values. I had not considered for a moment that the "American Way" may not work in a country whose largest population—its peasants and workers—were fervently religious and now heavily influenced by Khomeini's skill-fully crafted propaganda machine.

"We will do it our way," Sayed declared emphatically.

And, that was that. Our way. That was his humble plan. Those were his two words to sum up the cure for decades of political repression.

"Crazy," I muttered softly to myself.

. . .

Following the 1953 coup through the 1960s, Iran, like other post-WWII economies, grew at a comfortable pace. Oil revenues and "modernization" meant that factories were built while the country started to industrialize. The Shah implemented land reform programs that decimated Iran's agricultural self-sufficiency. By 1970, Iran saw a huge, bloated increase in middle managers and service jobs. These mid-level bureaucrats were paid large salaries, enjoyed lavish lifestyles and formed the core of the Shah's political base.

The Shah envisioned a newer, "richer" peasant benefiting from his state-sponsored break-up of the few, powerful landowners that controlled Iran's agriculture. His peasants would come to the cities and serve as his labor force. They would continue to industrialize and modernize the country. They would leave the sphere of influence of the clerics who ruled their villages. And so, in furtherance of this plan, farms were broken up and peasants, mainly single men of working age, migrated to the cities by the millions.

They came in waves. Mainly single men, they toiled in factories and on public work sites. The pay was minimal and the hours long. With little hopes of finding suitable brides and starting the good lives promised to them, men from very religiously conservative tiny villages, strolled through Tehran's public parks on their only days off, eyeing the modernized dress of the "new" Iranian woman with thinly veiled distain. Western style dress, restaurants, movies and shops sprung up like weeds to accommodate the newly affluent middle management class. By and large these places were out of reach or unattractive to the working men, who preferred the company of peers in traditional *gaveh khaneh* or coffee house, where women were not welcomed. These men were the backbone of the revolution. While the students spearheaded the movement, the real power fell to those disaffected elements.

. . .

I spent the rest of the Summer of 1978 traveling throughout the north and southwest of Iran. I visited the glorious city of Esfahān in the south. My father-in-law graciously drove his white Mercedes and acted as chauffeur, despite the fact that driving caused him enormous stress. We spent hours in the car, with me planted in the backseat and my nephew pointing out the sights as we passed. It was both serene and terrifying.

We traveled briskly along two-lane highways, passing trucks painted with brightly colored markings, decorated like moving Christmas trees. As Aghajune edged out into oncoming traffic, I would say a little silent prayer as he accelerated powerfully and slid back into our lane. Horns blared. My knuckles turned white. My father-in-law held his breath. It was truly an adventure.

Periodically, as we passed a truck, I looked up and saw the driver singing loudly along to music blaring from his radio or cassette player. There must be a universal rule that all long-haul truck drivers play loud music and have things hanging from their mirrors. These trucks were adorned with *Tass Bee*—worry beads. Introduced to Islam from the rosaries of Catholicism, these beads would wave back and forth from their positions around the rearview mirror.

Southern Iran looked exactly like I thought it would: an arid and dusty high desert with small villages dotting the sides of the roads. The homes were built with clay bricks and mud, and had domes perched atop the rounded roofs. They looked just as they had centuries before—sand-colored clusters of homes springing from the desert.

"The domes collect the breeze and circulate it through the home," my nephew announced with great pride. "They have built them this way for centuries."

Towns swallowed up the highway, forcing us to slow down to negotiate the twists and turns. The buildings were dull and unremarkable, and the streets were filled with men and women going about their business. Periodically we came upon some monument or park, slowing only briefly to allow me to take it in.

We arrived in Esfahān in the early evening. The city had not yet been fully illuminated with the strings of lights and signs that brighten most cityscapes in Iran. Esfahān was a busy city situated next to a beautiful rushing river spanned by ancient arched bridges. While the sun set over the river, families, groups of young men, and groups of women, walked arm-in-arm along the river walk.

Saturday was the only full day off in Iran. Shops closed early on Friday afternoons, a circumstance that was used later to attract thousands of the faithful to Friday prayer. Saturday was their weekend and the grassy gentle slopes overlooking the river were covered with picnickers—women passing out food, men smoking and congregating in small groups, children running down to the river to climb the rocks.

Esfahan is a gentle city full of history—a shining example of Persian pride. Its residents speak Farsi with a distinctive, almost melodic cadence. They are justifiably and fiercely proud of their city. It is located about 340 kilometers (211 miles) south of Tehran on the main north–south and east–west routes crossing Iran. It was once one of the largest cities in the world. It is famous for its Persian-Islamic architecture, with many beautiful boulevards, covered bridges, palaces, mosques, and minarets.

We stayed in a large, modern, and practically empty hotel. While checking in, my father-in-law was questioned at length about me—my purpose, our relationship. Ever vigilant to keep up the appearance of propriety in light of the growing, pre-revolution influence of Islamic morality, the desk clerk assigned me to a room on the opposite side of the almost-empty hotel. Thankful to be shown to my massive, modern room, I collapsed into bed.

The next morning, we toured the ancient palace of Ali Qapu, which overlooks Imam Square, an enormous area constructed centuries ago for games of polo. The Sheikh Lotfollah mosque sits facing the palace at the opposite end of the square. Built in the seventeenth century, the palace was a magnificent structure, a feat of advanced engineering. The outer borders of the square had given way to antique shops and tourist spots. Fake ivory miniatures illustrating ancient polo matches could be bought, along with standard postcards.

At night, we strolled down the main street to the river. We would stop and buy *bast tanee*, Iranian ice cream flavored with rosewater and squares of milk solids. The slight hint of saffron gave it a yellow tinge. It was refreshing and delicious.

This road trip was my gentle, unhurried introduction to Iran, the sights, the smells, the architecture and feel of towns and cities outside of Tehran. Sitting comfortably in the back seat of Aghajune's beloved Mercedes, I drank in the countryside one mile at a time.

The sightseeing gave me time to consider the real purpose of my trip. I thought of Hadj and how much he loved this country to which, at that time, he could not return. I thought of all of the hours, days, years Hadj had spent organizing, educating, cajoling and leading others towards that one, singular goal of a free and independent Iran. I felt strongly that I could not let him down. He needed me and it made me feel valued.

Hopes were high back in California and elsewhere that the growing wave of resistance and opposition to the Shah's regime would lead to its demise. It occurred to me as I sat there, gripping the armrest as Aghajune flew down the road, that no one I had every met in the resistance had really considered the hold that religion had on the people. There was always much talk about political oppression and fascism. Political campaigns had focused on exposing the torture and incarceration of opposition figures. But I had never, ever heard anyone take a long, honest look at how Islam shaped the thinking of the vast majority of the working poor in Iran.

Despite all of my good intentions and desire to impose my Western "revolutionary" agenda, it became increasingly clear to me that the Iranian student movement back home was painfully out of step with the reality of Khomeini's vision of the future and the impact this disillusioned single, displaced peasant workforce would have on Iran.

"We missed the boat," I thought.

I had come to Iran presuming that the struggle centered around human and political rights. I was learning quickly that it was the perceived rejection of non-Islamic ideals, that fueled this wildfire.

History tells us, of course, that we were totally caught off guard and ill prepared for what was to come.

CHAPTER 6
STUDENT OF CULTURE

Having eased into my stay with travels around the country, I now readied myself for my first large social engagement: Hossein's lavish wedding. Hossein's wedding was divided into two traditional parts: the engagement ceremony and the marriage portion. The engagement ceremony could take place a day or a year before the actual marriage. I, alas, missed the first event, but came toting my borrowed "long dress" for the second. I was ready to dress to impress!

I had come to Iran a Berkeley student with a suitcase full of jeans and casual shirts. At home I had nothing beyond this college-student uniform, and so I resorted to raiding my mother's closet before my trip. She was, after all, a grown up. Clearly, she would have a long dress for me to wear.

My mother had two choices: a pink, matronly two-piece ensemble that made me look vaguely like a church lady or a long white billowy gown covered with large red and pink roses; actually, very large red and pink roses. The billowy one had long sleeves and a collar, and I believe it was referred to as a shirtwaist gown. While it did not make me look like a church lady, trying it on and standing before a full-length mirror, I suddenly realized that I vaguely resembled a wounded wedding-cake topper from the 1950s. The prominent red and pink roses looked like gunshot wounds bleeding over the white expanse of the skirt. Undaunted and believing no one would really notice me or what I wore, I pulled it out of its protective plastic covering and threw it on.

I emerged from my room at my in-law's home, hair combed, dress donned, feeling anxious about the reception I would get from the crowd of female relatives who had gathered in the foyer waiting for my "reveal." Head held high and smiling broadly, I awaited what I had quietly prayed would be a shower of compliments.

"You like it? I borrowed it from my mother," I said, feigning confidence and enthusiasm. "Is it okay?"

I cannot adequately describe the look of abject horror that painted the faces of my Iranian in-laws as I stood before them dressed in my borrowed ball gown. My mother-in-law seemed to physically recoil as if she had discovered a corpse on her doorstep. She turned sharply toward her daughter and, with a hand over her mouth covering her shock, whispered something with apparent urgency.

It did not take long before it dawned on me that this dress, this expansive floral thing I wore, was not impressing anyone. Hadj's eldest sister, head bowed, leaned into Iranjune and whispered something that thankfully I could not understand at the time.

"Lisajune, you look...ah...nice," she lied.

It has now been over three decades since the dress debacle. Anytime I begin to reminisce about my days in Iran, someone (usually a sister-in-law, recently my niece) brings up that dress. They laugh so hard tears run down their faces.

At the appointed hour, we were chauffeured to what appeared to be some sort of private club nestled in the mountains that formed a crescent around northern Tehran. The venue was large and screamed expensive. Low chandeliers hung from the ceiling, casting a warm glow over the dozen or so tables covered with crisp white clothes.

Young men, dressed in spotless white uniforms and wearing white gloves, floated through the room with trays of wine glasses, cocktails or cigarettes.

The sound of a live band greeted me as I swished my way into the main hall. To my delight, the band seemed to be playing Beach Boys tunes with a relaxed, hip abandon, mispronouncing words and mangling phrases with adorable enthusiasm.

"Their English is better than my Farsi," I thought as I stood listening to the lead singer belting out, head back, eyes half closed: "Ah vish vee awl cood be Californ'a geerls." It was heaven.

Weddings in Iran can be enormously elaborate and expensive events. Despite taking place in a predominantly Muslim country, the ceremonies themselves date back to the pre-Isamic times of Zoroastrianism. The first portion is called the *Aghed*, which means knot. This is where the legal nuptials take place with both parties signing the formal marriage contract. The contract is supported by the *mehr*, which some in the West have mistakenly described as a dowry. The *mehr* is the bride's compensation for entering into the contract. It belongs to her and she may claim it anytime she wishes. It can be gold coins or furniture. Often a Koran is included.

The *Aghed* is done in a special room, ornately decorated with flowers and a cloth (*Sofreh*) on which a candelabra, sweets, flowers and a beautiful and elaborately decorated and spread on the floor. Traditionally it faced the direction of sunrise and, by custom, the event would normally take place at the bride's home or her close relatives and always during the day as during the Zoroastrian period darkness was associated with the hostile spirits. The bridegroom is the first to take his seat in the room and the bride comes afterward. The groom always sits on the right-hand side of the bride. With Zoroastrians, the right side designates a place of respect.

Food in enormous quantities filled the tables: rice shrouded by *tadeek*, the golden crust of rice created carefully and lovingly at the bottom of huge vats, with each tray of rice looking as if it were a molded gold mound; various *khoresh*, stew-type dishes; meats; chicken basted in saffron; piles of fruit extending high toward the ceiling; and breads and herbs and sweets and more rice and meat, more food than three times what the guests could eat, and all presented calculatingly to welcome and fill each guest. And, of course, there was booze. Wines and vodka, scotch if you insisted. Colas in actual bottles and other more traditional drinks filled the bar. It was a banquet of excesses in style and quantity.

Standing tall among the guests, I was not particularly well-versed in cocktail party chit-chat. My passionate involvement in social activism, coupled with my youth, made me exceedingly intense. Every social issue was magnified in scope and importance. Every conversation dedicated to winning over the skeptic to my particular view. My family often found it annoying as one might presume.

These people, dressed so elegantly who stood in small groups, sipping cocktails and listening to western music, they were not my people. And so, I spent a great deal of time nodding and smiling. While the guests were pleasant and polite, there was a distance between us. I was the American bride of the eldest son; the son who could not be there because of his politics.

"Oh, you are Mohamamad's wife," exclaimed the slim, manicured woman standing in front of me.

m his cousin's wife," she explained, motioning to a short,
nan sitting off to the side and deep in conversation, head
ispiratorially towards the man to his immediate right.

ı am," I replied, smiling.

"It is very sad he cannot be here," she offered. "We all support him, you know."

"Do you?" I responded reflexively. "Really? Come on…," I thought.

"Oh, yes. Although, for such a handsome man it is a shame that he has not done more with his life."

And, there is was. Who else in the room thought Hadj had "settled" when he married me? Did these people really see him as a failure?

"Whoa," I thought, "tough room."

It was imprudent to discuss politics in public during this period, and particularly at Hossein's wedding. Many of Hadj's relatives were either employed by the government or had become wealthy due to their connections to the regime. Contrary to the backhanded expression of "support" for Hadj, I doubted that I would find a truly sympathetic audience that night. And, frankly, I had no intention of pressing the issue. I was there as a guest.

The entire affair was so alien to me, literally and figuratively. The juxtaposition of the lavish reception with the social turmoil taking place outside the doors of the venue, made me uneasy. I had just returned from traveling around the country, having seen ornate, impressive buildings casting their long shadows over the blight urban poverty. I had driven through villages with homes made from the earth that surrounded them. But there I was mingling among the elite, keeping my mouth shut and smiling. It was a painful reminder of the reality of Iran's stratified society, where the vast majority lived in relative poverty and the very, very few controlled the wealth and power.

And there I stood, wearing that dress and sipping my cocktail, surrounded by the very people whose lives and livelihoods I believed would be irreparably changed by the cresting wave of the nascent revolution.

"Do they even have a clue?" I said to myself under my breath.

Finding myself momentarily overwhelmed, I quietly made my way out onto the nearest balcony, desperate for a cigarette and a moment of reflection.

"How are you finding Iran?" a voice behind me asked politely.

It was a simple, innocent, straightforward question and yet I struggled to answer.

"I find it confusing," I replied, turning to find another smoking companion had come outside in search of an ashtray.

"Well, we are a country of contradictions," he said, laughing softly as he crushed his cigarette butt into the edge of the balcony, nonchalantly tossed it on to the street and pivoted around to reenter the room, following the sound of the Beach Boys cover band playing loudly behind me.

Yes. Contradictions.

. . .

Four months after my arrival, my mission completed, I packed my suitcase and returned home. Anxious to share with Hadj my cautionary belief that the student movement needed to factor Khomeini into the equation, I breathlessly launched into my diatribe as I threw my suitcase into the back of our waiting car and jumped in beside him into the passenger seat.

Literally yelling over the sound of our tires as we flew down the freeway away from San Francisco International Airport and towards our home in Berkeley, my desire to impress my views on him was frantic and evangelical.

"Hadj! I am not kidding. You guys need to really pay more attention to Khomeini and this whole religious movement. The days of dismissing religion are done!"

I did not allow Hadj to get a word in edgewise, telling him about the Khomeini propaganda tapes and how they had been slowly and methodically influencing a mass of alienated working poor, and, had taken hold among university students and youth. I described to him in detail the atmosphere in Tehran. I admitted to him that I feared that the students outside of the country had lost touch with what was going on inside among their peers.

The Iranian student movement outside of Iran was populated by the children of parents not unlike the rich and privileged I had met at Hossein's wedding. These students were the elite few whose families could afford to send them across the world to foreign universities. These students became political outside of the direct and daily influences of Islam, unlike their counterparts who stayed to attend Tehran University and the like.

They were raised in households where prayer and Islam were, by and large, personal expressions of beliefs. Often, their mothers and sisters did not cover their heads and bodies with the *hijab* that would later become the mandatory dress for all women in Iran. Even in households where the fathers routinely attended prayers at the neighborhood mosque, the populations of those upper-class mosques were not the targets of politicized clerics. Those sermons were reserved for the working men and women; those sermons were contained in the tapes that my nephew so carefully retained and circulated.

While these students acknowledged that any inclusive Iranian version of democracy would need to include the voices of the peasantry and working people, they made students and intellectuals the focus of their organizing efforts outside of the country. They had no presence among those disaffected peasants who poured into the cities from the countryside looking for work and the hope of a better future.

Many of the most active students, those in the highest leadership positions, were most heavily influenced by Marxist and Maoist ideologies, which dismissed religion as the "opiate of the masses." While these student leaders recognized that a wholesale rejection of Islam would not fly in the villages of Iran as the clerics and mosques were far too entrenched in the day to day lives of the peasantry and working people, it appeared to me that they had no concrete plan of action.

"We cannot underestimate the hold that this religion has on people." This became my new mantra.

Entering the smoke-filled meeting room at the Iran House in Berkeley, Hadj and I each grabbed one of the chairs we found arranged in a neat circle. Various representatives of the organization's leadership, with their coffee in one hand and cigarettes in the other, assembled to hear me share my impressions.

Surrounded by the attentive and thoughtful audience and looking occasionally at Hadj for a sign of support, I launched into my narrative.

I repeated almost verbatim what I had told Hadj about Khomeini.

"He controls the narrative," I concluded.

"The great Satan is not just a catchy phrase," I declared. "It is their world view that subtly assigns a religious connotation to their enemy. But assigning an easy-to-remember phrase to the US,

Khomeini has given 'the enemy' an identifiable face. The US government is now a thing; a symbol. It's horribly brilliant," I concluded.

As the smoke from a half a dozen cigarettes curled through the stale air, my audience politely let me speak in wave after wave of impassioned declarations.

I was emphatic and preachy. I needed to be heard, believed. Instead, I was humored.

"Thank you, Lisa. We will keep this in mind," said the host.

"You do that," I thought. "You do just that."

At that time, Khomeini had yet to emerge on the international scene, for the general public, as the revolutionary leader he would eventually become. Prior to the revolution, the US had actually been in contact with Khomeini and continued to hear from him, secretly, up and until his eventual return to Iran. The *Guardian* newspaper disclosed in 2016 that in 1963 Khomeini contacted the US through an intermediary to offer assurances that he was not opposed to some US involvement in the country, and, that he believed that the US would serve as a buffer against the then Soviet Union and British attempts to assert their respective influence in the country.

Even on the eve of the revolution, Khomeini sought to assure the US that it should not fear his rise to the role of leader, replacing the Shah. But these contacts were secret and politically motivated and appeared to contradict his "Death to America" narrative.

Khomeini was not only a religious leader with a political agenda, he was an Iranian nationalist who sought, above all, to put what he viewed as the interest of the Iranian people above all else. Keenly aware that the US had, in the past and with the backing of Britain, changed the face of Iran's leadership with the 1953 CIA lead coup, Khomeini seemed willing to continue to co-exist in some form with US interests.

For the American viewing public, and Iranian the stude living outside of Iran and waiting to return, the Mike Walla Minutes" interview that aired in November 1979 would be their first, real introduction to Khomeini.

What was striking to Hadj and I as we sat in our small Berkeley apartment, glued to our black and white television, was that Khomeini had a real presence. He did not appear to be impressed by Wallace. He rarely made eye contact with him. It was less an interview *by* Mike Wallace and more of a private lecture *to* Mike Wallace. His words were simple and simply used. As a cleric, Khomeini was used to granting audiences to devoted adherents in an academic type setting. They would sit with him and listen as he espoused his views on Islam, politics and leadership. He had little experience with journalists, but managed to hold his own during the interview.

He also astutely understood the need to keep his message clear and simple. Over the years that followed, Hadj and I would hear him speak literally hundreds of times. His tactic was unmistakable: He would repeat a concept over and over, using clear and uncomplicated language; the language of the average, working person, until an idea was irreversibly planted into the mind of the listener. It was a brilliant strategy.

"Well?" I asked, leaning forward to turn off the television set. "What do you think?"

"Lisa*khanuum*," he started, his head lowered, slowly shaking it back and forth. "I am honestly not sure what to think," he admitted honestly.

"He has a real presence," Hadj continued. "He just seems above it all, as if Wallace was insignificant, almost annoying. He clearly knows how to use the media, though."

"What do you mean?" I asked.

"He could care less about Wallace. He doesn't care about television or any of that. He could care less about the power of the US. He is defying the world. It's hard not to be drawn to someone like him who tells the world 'screw you. We are in control now. We don't care about you. We are defiant."

"Can we work with these people?" I asked.

"We can try," his voice trailing. "We can try."

Neither of us were convinced.

CHAPTER 7
WHO'S IN CHARGE NOW?

The Iranian Revolution officially concluded on February 1, 1979, when the Ayatollah Khomeini returned to Tehran a triumphant leader. Stepping off his chartered flight at Tehran's international airport, the world watched as, clutching his robes against the wind, he slowly descended from his chartered jet onto the tarmac. In order to guard against the plane being sabotaged or shot down while on route, 120 foreign journalists were allowed to make the flight with him.

Nine months later, on November 4, 1979, a mob of Iranian students stormed the US embassy gates located on Takhte Jamshid Avenue, Tehran. They scaled the 20-foot walls and broke open the barred metal gates that led to the main embassy building. Facing overwhelming opposition and fearing for an irreparable international incident, the few brave US Marines guarding the embassy held their fire. No Iranians were killed during the assault, but a group of

American employees and embassy staffers were taken hostage. The world watched in horror as blindfolded Americans were led through a gauntlet of chanting protesters out of the main building to parts unknown. And, the American public joined in a nightly countdown. "Americans Held Hostage" was the headline. The nation was outraged.

But it was never that simple. The students targeted the embassy to demand that the Shah be returned to stand trial for his crimes against the Iranian people. President Jimmy Carter, citing "humanitarian reasons," allowed the Shah to enter the United States. To many commentators, it was as if he had thrown gasoline on a fire.

Initially, more than 60 Americans were held. Over time, some were released, bringing the final number of hostages to 52. Nightly news kept an ongoing tally of the days in captivity. Some Americans wrapped yellow ribbons around their trees to symbolize hope. Among others, anger rose like bile. Iranian students outside the country became the targets of harassment and physical attacks.

US embassies had been attacked before, but never had the attackers successfully invaded the sovereignty of a US embassy and held Americans captive. The world watched as the United States imposed political and economic sanctions on Iran—sanctions that have persisted in large part until quite recently. We were told Iran was the little country that took our people. We were told Iranians hated us, so we must, in turn, hate them.

By mid-December, 1979 I was asked by a coalition of groups to return to Tehran briefly as part of a delegation of Americans voicing support for the revolution and seeking the extradition of the Shah from the US back to the country he terrorized, to stand trial. We had no sympathy for his medical condition. He had brutalized a nation and needed to be held accountable for his crimes.

Along with an eclectic group of delegates comprised of an attorney, a feminist and her associate, a factory worker and noted student activists, we traveled to Iran to make some noise and raise some consciousness. I did not stay with my family during that trip, instead opting to remain simply the "Berkeley student" member of the group. I feared that any minor notoriety my presence back in the country might garner, would subject them to unnecessary scrutiny.

At the time, the press corp in Tehran was understandably pre-occupied with the embassy seizure and so our press conference, held at the Intercontinental Hotel in the north of the city, was sparsely attended. The US embassy had been overrun, people were being held hostage and no one really wanted to listen to a motley group of Americans voicing support for the revolution that precipitated that international crisis.

As a delegation, we traveled to the holy city of Qom to present a letter to Khomeini, who had offices there among the other religious leadership. Our letter was intended to let the nascent revolutionaries know that some Americans understood the history of US involvement in Iran and supported calls to extradite the Shah from the US, and, send him back to Iran to stand trial for his criminal excesses. We sent letters to the US embassies throughout the area as well, hoping to exert some small amount of influence.

We had hoped that any publicity surrounding our presence in Iran during that controversial time would cause the American public to begin to question what was going on in the country. It was a naive hope; we were no match for the wave of public opinion condemning the embassy seizure. The American people viewed the embassy sei-zure at a basic level: American citizens were being held hostage by a hostile government. It was seen as an unjustifiable, heinous act.

During those days, the streets surrounding the embassy com-pound were full of protesters and the hotels full of foreign journalists. It was a heady time for those of us who lived and breathed social change in Iran. Each day brought with it chaos and excitement. No one actually imagined that the hostage crisis would play itself out for over a year; and in our naïveté we presumed that the students would make their point and let everyone go. The seizure of the embassy would become a "grand gesture" followed by many strident press conferences denouncing something.

The US embassy in Tehran was a huge compound, at least one city-block wide and many blocks deep. It was a small, walled city housing a full-size football field, entire apartment complexes, outbuildings and barracks. It sat prominently on one of Tehran's busiest avenues, near the center of the city. Many people hold a belief that an embassy is a building whose primary function is to issue visas and renew passports. This is only partly true. Embassies are diplomatic outposts that exist, in large measure, to collect information. Not surprisingly, the US embassy had basements containing listening devices, satellite uplinks, telexes, and other forms of communication. While they did issue visas and helped out tourists, the embassy itself was all about national interests and information.

"Why did you do this?" I asked my nephew Sayed as we sat whispering conspiratorially, sipping tea in a hotel lobby near the embassy. "I mean, what can you guys possibly hope to gain from this?"

Reaching into his pants pocket, he produced a handful of matchbooks and slid them toward me with a grin. "United States Embassy, Tehran, Iran" was printed neatly in gold on white across the front. I grabbed them and thrust them into my purse.

"I have an ashtray, too. Souvenirs."

"So why?" I pestered.

Sayed had joined that first wave of students rushing the embassy compound. He stayed inside the compound, using his knowledge of English to serve as a translator. At first, he explained, it was just part of a protest to stop the United States from intervening after the Shah left the country. He was furious that the Shah had been invited to New York for medical treatment.

"Of course they brought him there. He works for them," he declared. "You know they tried to have political puppets take over for him. Bakhtiar was totally pro-American interests. That didn't work when the Ayatollah replaced him with Bazargan. It's our time now. We want them to know that we are in charge."

The Bakhtiar, to whom he referred, was the Prime Minister appointed immediately prior the Shah's departure to the US in late 1978 and early 1979. While appearing to work with the new revolutionary government, Bakhtiar was generally seen as a pro-US puppet. He was deposed within weeks and replaced by Khomeini with a more palatable Mehdi Bazargan,

Eyes down on the table, hands circling his small, glass cup of tea, "Listen, Lisa*june*" he said. "We had to do something. We showed them we are in control."

His pride was obvious. He and his friends, the students, had crippled the beast. No repeat of the 1953 coup, he bragged, "We hold all the cards now."

CHAPTER 8
IN BLACK AND WHITE

During my return visit in December 1979, I was contacted by a friend who thought it would be a great idea for us to check out what was happening at the US embassy. She was not a part of our delegation and had arrived in Iran from the United States many months before I did. A fearless adventurer, she had already scoped out the city. Together we would roam the streets in search of the best pizza or the best cup of coffee. Tehran was actually mapped out for me by food groups. In our strange pidgin Farsi, we would speak in food code over the phone to arrange meetings.

"Meet me at the ice cream place with the real stuff."

"See you at the pizza place with the real cheese."

I knew exactly where these places were and what she meant.

"Let's go to the embassy," she declared one day over a plate of rice and *chelokabab*.

"Sure. Why not?" I glibly replied.

About a quarter of a million people were standing in front of the US embassy compound on the day that she and I, carrying a dozen red roses we thought we should bring, decided to pay our visit. Images of thousands of chanting protesters burning American flags and screaming *"Marg ba Amrika"* (Death to America) were the daily meat and potatoes of broadcast news in the West. I knew this because those pictures and the accompanying sound bites terrified my poor parents. They sat at home watching the nightly news, wondering where they had gone wrong. What was their daughter thinking living in that place?

One could not simply take a taxi to the front gate of the embassy. The broad avenue in front of the main entrance had been closed off so we approached on foot, having met several blocks to the west. As we neared the crowds, my heart began to race with excitement at the sight of the sea of humanity shifting like a strange dark tide pressing forward to allow closer access to a view of the barricaded front gate.

We tended to be oblivious adventurers and so it never once dawned on either of us that we would be in any danger from this massive crowd. We understood that we were of absolutely no consequence to anyone. We had no official standing and no real agenda beyond just being there. We were more like tourists than political observers. And so we charged ahead fearlessly with an abundance of confidence.

"We brought flowers," I announced to the Revolutionary Guard who approached us as we neared the barricade separating the world from the front gate of the US embassy compound. Holding them up in the air like an Olympic torch, I waived the bouquet back and forth as if to signal. The guard stood before us, erect, and slowly lowered his weapon to his side.

"We are Americans," I said with that silly mix of confidence and arrogance usually reserved for people waving foam fingers over their heads at sporting events.

We had, of course, fully expected to make a showy presentation of our roses to the guards and then be asked to politely leave. However, remarkably and to our complete surprise, the guard motioned us forward toward another group of armed sentries.

Perhaps it was our strange appearance that intrigued them. I am an almost-six-foot-tall, blue-eyed American woman dressed in jeans, clogs, and a jaunty blue head scarf. My friend was a tiny version of me in her navy blue overcoat and winning smile. Regardless, we snaked through the throng of curious armed guards toward the unit apparently charged with access to the embassy.

I should note here that while the embassy was overrun by students, the regime began the process of systematically replacing the student leaders with more "professional" soldiers in the form of Revolutionary Guards who stood watch outside. With their brand-new uniforms and AK-47s slung over their shoulders, these men patrolled the perimeters of the compound and manned the no-man's-land between the hoard of demonstrators, the foreign press, and the front gate of the embassy.

We moved toward the Revolutionary Guards milling about the barricade. With our "Hell, why not?" attitude and feigned sense of urgency, we informed them we needed to cross the barrier and see the students.

The barricade that separated the avenue, with its hundreds of thousands of milling supporters, and the steel bars of the front gate of the embassy compound was comprised of wood and wire. It was approximately six-to-eight feet wide and easily as tall. The guards had fashioned a crossing that was up, across, and down the barricade. I was completely taken aback at the ease with which they allowed us over that barricade. At the time, I just assumed we were official-sounding enough to pass inspection. To this day, I have no idea why and how it all happened.

Parting like the Red Sea, the mass of guards allowed us to step quickly through their ranks and maneuver our way gracelessly up, over, and down onto the sidewalk below. Once on the other side, we stood alone on the expansive sidewalk, our backs to a quarter of a million people.

There is nothing I can say to describe what it feels like to stand in front of a quarter of a million people and to feel the gaze of hundreds of thousands of eyes boring into your back. Unsure of the reactions or actions of the protesters, I kept my eyes glued on the embassy building and avoided turning to face them. I could hear the sounds of shutters clicking, vague calls out to us from members of the media. We purposely shunned any attempt to get our attention, so it was surprising to us that after we clambered out of the area, no journalist bothered to ask us who we were and what we thought we were doing there that day.

We stood there at the front gate of the embassy compound absorbing the energy of the crowd and peering hopefully through the bars of the metal gates. Several minutes passed. At last a small woman wearing a navy blue hijab emerged from out of the guardhouse to the right of the gate.

"Can I help you?" she asked in English, quizzically.

Her English was excellent and her name was Maryam, we later discovered. As a representative of the students in the embassy, she would appear regularly at televised press conferences, head bowed and reading mechanically from a prepared statement in English; her speech slow and deliberate.

We asked her about the seizure of the embassy: why, how, who. She answered frankly and honestly. She reiterated what my nephew had already told me, that the students had demanded the Shah be returned to Iran to be held accountable for his transgressions and that they believed another coup to overthrow Khomeini was in the works. We asked how long they would remain. She didn't know.

Returning to the guardhouse to the right of the gate, she came back quickly carrying a small bound package. It was a stack of papers comprised of copies of memos and telegrams the students had meticulously pieced together from those documents, hastily shredded by embassy staff members as the embassy was overrun.

"Look at these," she asked as she handed me the bundle of papers. "They will show you what was really going on here. Tell people about them. Show the American people these. Tell them we have nothing against them. This is about foreign policy."

Assuring her that we would do what we could, I clasped the documents tightly to my chest. I had no way of knowing then that I would sometime later travel around the United States, giving speeches at universities, in churches, and the like, sharing these documents with as many people as I could in an effort to make some sense of the actions of those students that day in November 1979.

The 1970s were the days when information was transmitted by telex, telephone, and telegraph. Information was produced and maintained in hard copy and thus paper trails were created that had to be covered up. It came as no surprise that when the students took over the embassy they discovered the piles of shredded documents shoved into bags as yet unburned and began the laborious process of piecing these shreds together to form documents.

While this process was extremely time-consuming, in the end the students were able to piece together just enough information to support their belief that the United States was, again, conspiring to destabilize the nascent Khomeini government, as it had when it orchestrated the CIA coup in 1953. There were plans to ruin the economy by flooding the market with counterfeit cash. There were discussions of bribes and buying influence—all of it in black and white. These documents revealed the United States had hopes to interfere and intervene. All of it added fuel to the fire that was the Islamic Revolution. This was the rationalization for taking the US embassy. The students felt they were stopping yet another US-led coup.

Our encounter at the embassy was only minutes long, but the mark it left on each of us was indelible. We had met history, shook its hand, and presented it with flowers. While we asked a few broad, general questions and got answers as equally noncommittal, we knew that we had been privileged to literally cross a barrier toward a better understanding of the motivation behind such a remarkable event.

CHAPTER 9
SPREADING THE TRUTH

Upon my return from that delegation, in January 1980, I travelled across the United States, spreading my message and trying to explain why the embassy was seized as best I could. I had hoped to give some context to the recent events in Iran and hopefully enlighten supporters and detractors alike. I felt that Americans both demanded and deserved to know why the students felt compelled to seize the embassy. I wanted to share with them my nephew's perspective, the history of the US involvement in Iran and the fear that the 1979 revolution would prompt a repeat of the 1953 coup. I had a point of view. Mine were not "objective" talks; I was a militant advocate who hoped against hope that a progressive government offering personal freedoms would emerge from the powerful regime change that occurred that cold February day when Khomeini's plane touched the tarmac.

I traveled from San Francisco to Los Angeles, to Austin, Texas to Houston, Texas. Next, I landed in Birmingham, Alabama then shot up to Madison, Wisconsin, Detroit, Michigan, Chicago, Illinois. I finished up touring the Pacific Northwest and as a bonus, booked a week of speeches in Honolulu, Hawaii.

During this time, Hadj was still in Berkeley working behind the scenes as he did, anxiously monitoring the day-to-day politics and conscious of any shifts and changes. He was a coalition builder by nature, and so he did what he did best: Worked to educate; inform and build support.

Flying into a new city, I would speak on morning radio or television talk shows, attend receptions organized by supporters. The evenings, I spoke on the radio and fielded hostile questions from radio announcers. I was interviewed on television and in the newspapers. I gave speeches in churches and in the lecture halls of colleges and universities. I attended receptions given by wealthy progressives and potlucks at inner-city churches.

When I would speak at a hall, a church, or in a classroom, the attendees' donations would buy me a ticket to my next stop. All of this was, of course, organized by a coalition of progressives and radicals. The word about Iran, the revolution and the embassy seizure needed to get out, and I was the messenger. Don't shoot me.

I had virtually no money to spend, so volunteers made a place for me in spare rooms and sofa beds. I would arrive, blurry eyed and exhausted from a day of speeches and programs and fall into bed.

Three decades later, the details of these trips are a blur. I am sure some of the names, places, and events may be a tad off. At each stop, I would be met at the airport by a volunteer bodyguard. (It is ironic that I had come from a country where the people had a reason to hate me, yet back in my own country I was subjected regularly to death threats. Land of the free, home of the intolerant?) I would land and find the two large men—of whom I referred generically as Big Mike and Big Bob—holding a sign at baggage claim with Lisa R. printed on it. I'd get in a car and be driven to a radio or television station for a live on-air interview. The questions were the same everywhere. My responses were the same everywhere. They treated me with vague interest. I would finish and be off to the next appointment. At night I gave the big speech, answered questions, or went to a reception for a little one-on-one time with folks. This was, of course, followed by late-night radio, and then it was off to the airport to start again.

I recall one rather amusing television interview in Texas, perhaps Dallas or Houston. I know it wasn't Austin (the Berkeley of the south). It was a show called, "Mornings with Peggy Sue" (or was it Betty Sue or Missy Sue?). At any rate, it was a morning talk show, and the hostess was a lovely middle-aged woman with a huge puff of blond hair, a wide smile, and a soft Texas drawl. This was not the hard-news format I thought I'd be doing, and I feared just for a moment that we'd have to whip up a batch of cookies together. Nope. She let me talk. She started off after introducing me by asking, "So tell me, what are you here to talk about?"

Sadly, by the time I had hit Texas, I had said the same thing many times over: "I'm here to educate the American people...1953 coup...the Shah...undue US influence...hostages at the embassy... overthrow Khomeini...we may not like him, but shouldn't we let the Iranian people control their own fate?"

It probably came off a little canned. But Betty or Peggy or Missy Sue just sat across from me and smiled broadly as I spoke.

After allowing me to do my entire spiel, she said—again with a huge smile and soft southern tones, "Well, young lady, I cannot believe you have just said those terrible things about our government on my show. I just bet our viewers would like to string you up about now." Huge, warm, fuzzy smile—last line delivered directly into camera.

Thankfully, for every Betty Sue there were several others who really appreciated the message. People who came up to me later and claimed I had changed their lives in some way.

After each and every public event, I would wait and take questions from the audience. The questions and comments were intense. People had been moved, they told me. They were now ashamed of what had been done in their names in the past. They were activated by my words. Some declared they had been transformed forever.

I realized they were caught up in the emotion of the moment. They had come because they already had an interest and thus they were already halfway to a conversion experience before they even sat down. I knew my impassioned speech could put them over the edge, as it were, and turn them into the advocates I wanted them to be.

But I was not going for shame. I did not want people ashamed. That was not the point. We are blessed to live in a free society. We need to appreciate that. We are blessed to live in a society where our ideas may not only be expressed but are protected. We have the US Constitution. Most of the world does not have anything like it. I wanted them to leave feeling outraged— feeling the need to proselytize others—to share my story and the story of the Iranian people with anyone who would listen.

On one memorable occasion, I spoke at a college campus somewhere in the Midwest. It was a large lecture hall, and I was happy to see it almost completely filled. My bodyguards—Big Mike/Big Bob—had told me some students on the campus, having heard of my arrival, had organized a protest.

"We think some of them are here tonight," Big Mike said to me. "If anything at all happens, duck behind the podium and just stay there." Fun.

I gave my speech that night without incident. I asked for questions from the audience, expecting hecklers, but none emerged. I was sure the opposition had not bothered to show up. After the presentation, as usual, I hung back. Sitting on the edge of the stage, I waited to be approached by the shy ones who could not bring themselves to ask questions openly. A few people came up to me. Their questions were the same ones I had answered before—all but one.

I noticed a young man hanging back, waiting for the others to leave. Once I was free and alone, he approached me. With tears welling up in his eyes and head bowed, he said, "I want to let you know that I came here tonight to ruin this. My friends and I—we made fliers and stuff against you. I thought you were gonna say a bunch of crap. I thought you were a traitor. You changed my mind. You changed me."

I was very touched by his honesty.

"I never knew any of this stuff before," he said. "I never really thought about it. I am angry now. I feel like my emotions have been manipulated by the media. I feel like someone's been lying to me."

It was an awakening for him. I recognized his emotions. I too had been awakened once. I too had felt I was being deceived. I too had those tears in my eyes. I knew how he felt. I told him to go and learn and tell others. I told him he just had to make sure he did his homework.

"Don't go around saying the United States sucks," I said. "That's stupid. It doesn't. We have so much here; so much. I can give my speeches without worrying about being arrested. That's huge."

"But what about taking hostages? Do you support that?"

"Of course not," I replied, emphatically, "I don't support the act," I explained, "but I understand the reasoning. They are prisoners of war; a silent war, but war nonetheless."

Those were the early days of the revolution when my hopes for social change were optimistic, albeit cautious. We still had no idea what kind of country Iran would become under Khomeini, but held onto high hopes that he would make the reforms. We did not know how we would fit into the Islamic Republic either. Would the clerics allow differing points of view to co-exist? Had the window of free speech and thought cracked upon enough to allow a narrow beam of light to shine?

It was time for Hadj and I to return to Iran to build our new lives there. I could not escape my fears and trepidation about leaving the comfort and ease of my life in California. Hadj, too, acknowledged he had no real answers.

"It is just time to go back" he announced.

Our fears and excitement weighed heavily upon us as we began the arduous process of packing our modest belongings into suitcases. With hearts racing and hopes soaring, we boarded our flight and set off to make our new life in Iran. Holding hands as the plane ascended into the skies over San Francisco, I turned to see Hadj quietly and unapologetically weeping.

CHAPTER 10
RETURNING HOME

"I have come back after twenty years," Hadj announced, throat heavy with emotion, to the female customs agent at the airport the day we landed. "I have come back. Home."

And, with that she did not even bother to look in our bags. She smiled broadly at him and declared, "Welcome."

It was early 1980 and Hadj's head was spinning with excitement. So much had changed for him during those twenty years. He had left Iran as a very young man, left on his own to make choices that would form his adult personality. He was fiercely loyal to his people and yet would discover that he could only eschew many of what he felt were "backward" cultural norms. Over time, he found himself more and more pulled between two cultures.

But, on that day as our plane descended into the grey haze of Tehran's international airport; at that moment while we waited silently to board shuttle buses to the terminal; at that single instant when he stepped through the sliding glass doors leading into the building; on that day that he touched Iranian soil for the first time in decades, he was fully, completely and joyfully 100 percent Iranian.

We arrived to tears and kisses and much merriment. The prodigal son had returned and the family was over the moon.

It did not take Hadj long to settle into our life in Tehran. He was home and all that was unfamiliar and foreign to me, was like breathing to him.

"I never feel like I really belong," Hadj had confided to me one day in California. "I always feel a little out of balance here. I will never feel American".

Coming home at last, Hadj hoped to regain that "balance" he so missed in California.

We took up residence in that studio apartment at the back of the family home and spent the first few months enjoying Iranjune's and Aghajune's company. I spent my time sitting in the kitchen with Iranjune while she laboriously prepared food and trying to communicate with her with a mix of slowly articulated English and hand gestures. I now recall these moments spent with Iranjune with great fondness. Over time, as my Farsi improved, I came to appreciate her keen sense of humor and compassion expressed as we sat together cleaning pebbles from the rice. Pouring cups of the long, hard grains of fragrant Basmati rice onto large, aluminum trays, we would carefully and meticulously separate the grains, a few at a time, in such a way as to allow us to isolate and remove the pebbles invariably found within. Guests of a lazy cook invariably risked a broken tooth if the rice were poorly cleaned. Iranjune was not lazy.

For his part, Hadj immediately contacted his comrades and began his work secretly organizing "the masses" to further press for progressive, democratic social change. Their goal was a form of socialized democracy, founded on the belief that the people should control their own social, economic, and cultural fate. While spending decades working with the ISA, Hadj's own political affiliations were more radical and Marxist than the principles around which the ISA had been organized. He and his cohorts envisioned a true Democratic Socialism in Iran. And, while he did not shy away from espousing these views, the majority of ISA members were somewhat less radicalized. They just wanted freedom. Simple.

The advent of Khomeini, taking Hadj by surprise, gave rise to the new reality of the Islamic Revolution. It posed real challenges for Hadj and his comrades. As a natural organizer, Hadj sincerely believed that the people would come to see the benefits of a democracy that adopted many of the socialist principles of universal education, health care, gender equality and the like. A little vague on the specifics of how to accomplish this new mandate, the work now centered on lessening the hold of Islam on regular working people and promoting the idea that they themselves should be able to elect representatives who would promote public programs that would benefit them. It would be a hard sell.

Women would form groups dedicated to public health, child care, and educational issues, building ties between decidedly middle-class educated students and poor working people. The "indoctrination" was subtle and slow and always tied to the underlying belief that socialized democracy would make Iran independent and free.

Each morning, I knew that when Hadj walked out the front door he was secretly meeting with his comrades, making plans, making contacts. And, each morning I knew that he might never return, having been swept up by the regime's secret police.

For my personal safety I had no idea who or why or where. If detained, I would have no information to divulge. We never, ever spoke of any of it in front of anyone in his family, particularly his

parents. It was a need-to-know situation and I had absolutely no
to know anything. We posed as regular folk; a married couple ju
ing our lives. He would be our provider. He had things to do and that
I would amuse myself settling into Iranian life.

For a brief period after the revolution, newspapers and public political debate flourished. Groups of men, intently arguing with
cigarettes hanging from their lips, could be found on street corners,
at universities, or public coffee houses. The atmosphere was electric
and thrilling. For the first time in their lives, people seemed to want to
actually have a voice in what would be their futures. This appearance
of "freedom" was short lived, sadly.

True Democracy is not a genetically inherited trait. One is not
born knowing how to act using its principles. It is a learned political
system and the Iranian people, after literally decades of repression,
had not even learned to crawl. As they struggled to understand it and
how they could shape the future of the country, the population experienced temporarily at least a few more freedoms than they had ever
had in the past. In direct response, the new regime, realizing it must
control its own agenda and the political narrative, quickly moved to
quash all free expressions of idea.

It became a dangerous time, however, after the revolution for
people espousing ideas that challenged those of the ruling "Party of
God." Among the ruling elite were factions and contenders. Dissenters
were summarily executed, even among ministers and previously powerful public figures. The Islamic Republic was in a state of constant
flux, with moderates rising and falling out of favor within days at
a time.

It was also a time when the people were bombarded with mes-
sages of fear. Invading ideologies, they were told, would threatened
the republic. Everyone must spy on his or her neighbor. Being an
officious intermeddler was seen as heroic. Even our trash collector

watched our trash. It was serious business and anyone involved in any manner in any sort of political activity was placed at actual risk of death.

Back in California, when Hadj's political activism had been reported to the secret police through spies sent to monitor the students in California, Hadj's father was hauled into an interrogation with SAVAK. Aghajune was not a brave man and he could never get over the terror and indignity of it. Hadj carried around significant guilt over this, but he continued on with his work, believing that the movement's goals outweighed personal risk.

And so, once we had settled nicely into the flow of daily life, Aghajune announced it was time for him and Iranjune to hit the road. They had a small apartment in Geneva where they would stay for a while each year while visiting Hadj's sister, who lived there. After Geneva, they would continue on to California, where they took up residence with Hadj's sister, the doctor.

We had the house to ourselves and they had no fear of visits from the authorities. It was a win-win.

CHAPTER 11
FINDING HAPPINESS AMONG FIFTH-GRADERS

Within a few months of our arrival, Hadj and his comrades had begun the process of planning for a business of their own. It would be a cover they could use to shield their political activities and to justify their presence floating among the working people found in the south of the city.

Hadj would get up at dawn each day, dress as casually and inconspicuously as he could in a pair of old gray slacks and a buttoned-down blue shirt. He began to grow the short, unkempt stubble of the beard that marked a "true believer." Careful to wear Iranian-made shoes and a simple overcoat so as to fit in, he would walk out of our lovely home in the affluent northern section of town to take a one-hour bus ride to the dusty, crumbling working-class southern neighborhood that would house his new factory.

"The hardest part is that after all these years outside of the country, I have forgotten a lot of words," Hadj would tell me. "I have to watch what I say, even looking the part," he cautioned.

The southern neighborhoods of the city, as far as one could go from the mansions and cool breezes of the north's mulberry tree-lined streets, were home to Tehran's poor and working poor. Just outside of the most southern border, on a plot of land surrounded by a low mud fence, stood two long, rectangular buildings. They were made of stone and stucco and were the color of the sandy dirt on which they stood. Large enough to contain a small manufacturing facility, the buildings possessed the two necessities for any enterprise: power and water.

The land and the two buildings themselves belonged to Aghajune, who had purchased them many years before and let them stand empty. With his permission, Hadj had commandeered it as a place in which to build a business, and, more importantly, be in, around, and near everyday working people. Aghajune had, of course, no idea that the land and buildings would be used as a base for Hadj and his comrades' political activism. He was told it would be a factory, and a factory it indeed eventually came to be.

Organizing and educating working people about secular democracy was Hadj's new mandate, a purpose that he embraced with the same enthusiasm and energy he did working with organizations and churches in the United States. In Iran, however, the stakes were high and the dangers very, very real. Community organizers had to be exceedingly subtle and the pace was excruciatingly slow. Hadj found that those working men with whom he ate a delicious and basic lamb and chickpea stew called *abgusht* ("water/meat") were standoffish. As a new neighbor appearing seemingly out of nowhere in that working-class section of town, he was met with a mix of ambivalence, suspicion, and curiosity.

Unlike California, where political organizers merely printed fliers and handed them out on street corners, Hadj and his cohorts had to slowly vet each and every new contact. Feeling out a person with antifundamentalist sympathies, while making sure he was not an informer, required patience and resolve. Each new recruit had the potential to turn Hadj into the SAVAMA, the new secret police who had taken over all but the name of the previous organization of SAVAK. Pushing for social change in that atmosphere meant risking one's life, not simply a night in jail, as had been the case in California.

It was exhausting work and it required enormous patience. For Hadj, it was a constant challenge. After all, he had waited two decades to return to his homeland. He had been filled with an abundance of enthusiasm and hope that a real democracy and real social freedom would be possible in Iran. But when he finally returned, he found that the time away had Westernized him. He forgot words. He caught himself reflexively dismissing social norms, only to be harshly reminded by his companions that this would be the surest way to have him stick out among the "locals."

"We will build a factory in the neighborhood, Lisa*Khanuum*," he declared one night as we sat over our meal of rice and lentils. "We have decided to make electric heaters. It will take a lot of time to get the project off the ground," he admitted. "I am not sure I remember all the words in Farsi for the parts!"

The November 4, 1979 takeover of the US Embassy and the resultant economic embargo had forced fuel and food rationing in Iran. The start of the Iran-Iraq war on September 22, 1980 further exacerbated these shortages. Oil and gas were distributed via coupons issued to each household. It was, of course, the height of irony that one of the greatest oil-producing countries in the world forced its citizens to queue up with ration cards in order to fill up a tank.

Hadj and his crew therefore decided that producing safe, inexpensive electric space heaters would be an excellent project for their factory. They bought one from a Chinese competitor, and with wonderful ingenuity took it apart piece by piece so that they could copy it.

Parts had to be sourced locally, and Hadj experienced firsthand the dubious joy of trying to do business in a society where things are just not done as efficiently as one would hope.

"Lisa*june*," he exclaimed, the exasperation starkly evident in his voice. "You know I have discovered that in business here the word *fardah* (tomorrow) means anytime between now and the end of time as we know it!"

The business practice was always the same: Go to the office of the supplier. Sit with him in his office, accept and drink tea, discuss the weather, poetry, an illness, anything but the reason for the visit. After wasting an hour or so on superfluous small talk, finally get to the point. It was a slow and torturous dance that had become alien to Hadj.

"It takes hours to place an order," he complained, shaking his head back and forth slowly to illustrate his frustration. "Hours!"

After months of meeting with suppliers from the bazaar, agonizing over designs and planning assembly, Hadj's factory/front began production. The company's name, "Avaline," meant "first" and "best." And for Hadj, it was.

I, too, needed a purpose so I applied for a job as a schoolteacher for the Ministry of Education. The pay was terrific, my American friends had told me. The government had set a salary cap and school teachers at the international school where I applied to work earned exactly the same amount as the president of the country: 7,000 tomans a month—at that time, the spending equivalent $3,000 a month today.

I had absolutely no training as a schoolteacher. I was a UC Berkeley graduate with a bachelor's degree in French literature. I had never thought of teaching before and had no idea how to do it.

With a "hell, why not?" bravado, I presented myself one morning at the international school in the west of the city and lied. I handed the newly installed headmaster of what was formerly an elite international school a teaching credential I had forged carefully on my IBM Selectric typewriter. A precursor of the computer, the remarkable IBM Selectric, allowed the user to change type fonts by replacing the small font ball cartridges located within its carriage. I had brought with me a bunch of different font balls that I had used to fabricate an official-looking letter that stated I was credentialed to teach in California. I took a salt shaker, inked the bottom of it with an ink pad, and stamped the bottom right-hand quadrant of the document.

Most people in the developing world love documents that appear to be officially stamped in some manner. My document looked good, except if you held it up to a mirror and read the seal you would have seen "Made in Japan" in mottled blue ink.

Aarmed with my forgery, I headed to the principal's office at Iranzamin School in the West City portion of Tehran.

The administrative offices of Iranzamin were bustling with predominantly foreign women coming and going. Eventually I talked myself into the office of the headmaster, a lovely man who was cheerful and clueless. I have no idea how he ended up in charge of the school but assumed he was just a well-connected follower of Khomeini. It was apparent to me and everyone else there that he was hopeless and clearly terrified of messing up his new job.

"I would like a job," I said in English as I slipped my forgery across his desk.

His knowledge of English seemed very limited and I was confident that he had no idea what the document actually said.

"Can you start tomorrow? We need teachers." And so began my new career.

Iranzamin School was a bilingual school serving children from elementary grades through high school. Before the revolution it had been an international school run by an American and offering International Baccalaureate degrees for the children of American military personnel and others. After the revolution, management and control of the school had been taken from its board of trustees and placed in the hands of a revolutionary board.

By the time I started to work there, it had been transformed into a boys-only school, where sons of Iranians who had fled the Shah (or who had been born outside of Iran and did not speak Farsi) attended the school. We had a parallel teaching program that I never really understood. We foreigners would teach our classes in English, and later the same day the children would attend classes in Farsi. I figured our Iranian counterparts were teaching them some of what I taught, but frankly, I had no way of knowing. The Farsi teachers and the English-speaking ones never compared notes. We never exchanged lesson plans. We actually rarely, if ever, spoke.

The school employed a number of foreign-born teachers: American, German, Indian, and French. The building had been designed by a Westerner, and it looked like every high school I have ever seen in California. The former football fields were gone and all that remained was a huge Quonset hut that had once been used as a gym. It gave the campus the unfortunate appearance of a military installation.

In addition to faculty from the United States, Europe, and the Near East, the school's administrative staff included "morality" police hired to preserve the moral character of the students. During the

Shah's time, schools also had monitors who supervised the children moving from class to class and doled out discipline when needed. Our monitors took that function a little further and were there to make sure that none of our foreign immorality rubbed off on the kids. It was, after all, an all-boys school that employed women.

My kids were terrific co-conspirators in my attempts to mess with the monitors. I would have my "Student of the Week" sit near the classroom door. When the monitor would come by to spy on my class, he would do so with his ever-present cigarette hanging from his lips. As a result, his cigarette smoke would waft through the suspicious holes in the door right into my classroom.

The honored student was allowed to throw open the door, catching the monitor in the act of spying. Once caught with that deer-in-the-headlights look—the entire class would declare in unison, "*Salaam Agha!*" (Hello, sir!). Then we would close the door and laugh riotously. It was great fun.

I loved being a teacher, although I was often terrified. The kids were hard to fool. And they never missed a beat. In my class, a child got a gold star if he discovered a spelling mistake on one of my handouts. It was not unheard of in those days for me to butcher a word. There was no *spellcheck* on the mimeograph machine.

I had one set of concerned parents come to me because their son had reported that I told him to put his socks in his mouth. In my defense, I had actually said to him, "Reza, take off your shoes. Now take off your socks and stuff them in your mouth!" He was a chatterbox. He did not, of course, actually put his socks in his mouth. It was a joke and he had gotten the point.

He reported this exchange to his parents. Having never actually been a teacher, I had no idea what to say to them when they came to see me for a conference. These parents were used to attending parent-teacher days in Orange County, California. I suspect they thought I might have some semblance of training. When they pointed out my misspellings, I lied and said it was my way of making sure the children were, in fact, reading the material. I could not bring myself to confess to them that I had no idea what I was doing.

I figured I could deal with a room full of sixth graders, but I ended up frantically keeping one step ahead of my boys by reading the chapters the night before, making notes on cards, and trying to really teach them something.

The sciences were my favorite subject, and we began a curriculum on evolution. We created a new planet called Gazinka. This planet, populated by species of animals that were somewhat like those found on Earth, was our vacation retreat.

I would have the boys sit with eyes closed, put their thumbs in their ears and thus create little antennae while we traveled in our spaceship to Gazinka. Then after we had pushed the desks off to the side, we would walk around the room pointing out the imaginary animals we could see.

"Look!" shouted one student in glee. "I see an animal with no backbone." Impressive, eh?

I would say, "On Earth, what would we call this animal?"

And then the kids would guess. It was a great game. It allowed my boys to move around using their imaginations and learning at the same time. It was very different from the system of learning in Iran, which was to teach by rote memorization and copy from one textbook into another.

The old Iranian system works for them. The students excel in math and science. But I was dedicated to rebelling against the system, any system. So, with no prior teaching experience, I decided that rote memorization and repetition was wrong.

My kids were funny, smart and talented. They were also very, very impressionable. I liked that a lot. I would tell them half-jokingly that if I got fired for any reason, they had to stop "business as usual" at the school and protest to get me back. I did fear that I'd be let go. The school board was vacillating between conservative and centrist policies. We were sure they were going to come down with some rule prohibiting foreigners teaching their kids.

During my first year of teaching, I became ill and had to take a week off. Thinking I had been fired, my boys, bless them, made little picket signs and marched around the quad. They threw paper airplanes at the substitute with slogans written on them. The headmaster was called to my classroom and they bombarded him with airplanes and wadded-up paper, chanting, "We are the soldiers of Ms. Lisa!"

Finally, out of desperation, the headmaster called me at home.

"When will you be better?" he asked, tensely. "How long will you be out?"

I told him I was ready to return.

"Well," he sighed, relieved, "thanks be to God. Your boys are out of control. But," he continued, "we have another problem. The ministry has said women may not teach boys above the fifth grade. I have to move you from your sixth graders. I have a third-grade class opening. Are you interested?"

"Sure, I am," I told him. I had grown to love the job.

"But you must do something for me, *Khanuum*. You must go to the children and explain to them you have chosen to leave and teach the third grade. You must stop the protests. They are out of control." He was desperate.

"I will go one better," I replied. "I have my own replacement. I will bring in a new teacher—a man—and introduce him to the boys.

They will love him. He's an engineer, US trained, very smart, of course. You will like him."

Because the pay was so generous, I had no trouble finding one of Hadj's friends to come in and take over for me. On his first day, I took him into the classroom. He stood there looking amazed as the boys stood and cheered.

"Our teacher has returned!" they yelled in unison.

I explained to them that I had brought them a man, and that men were now required to teach little men, and that he was a good friend of mine.

"Treat him as you would treat me," I cautioned. "Or else!"

I found teaching third grade far less taxing than the older boys. I had ninety stinky little boys crammed into one large room. My primary challenge, as they sat side by side, became stopping them from poking one another. The close proximity, the constant unrelenting contact, created a veritable petri dish of germs that spread flus and viruses like a prairie fire throughout the classroom. And then there was the lice.

My goal of course was to get through each day without touching a single child. Small victories, small rewards.

CHAPTER 12
THE COMPLEXITIES OF GROCERY SHOPPING

Thankfully still untouched by the fluidity of Iranian politics as we went about building our lives, we continued to live with as much normalcy as we could muster. Life goes on. Family offers comforts. Some of my fondest memories of my time in Tehran were the warm nights spent sitting outside on our marble terrace, sipping tea, and eating cucumbers. The family would congregate and sit laughing and talking. In the background, wafting through the mulberry and saffron trees came the sound of the call to prayers flowing from the nearby minaret, those singular male voices singing notes that appear to last for minutes, calling, attracting, and beseeching the faithful to prayers.

The songs in Arabic, the language of Islam, were softened to attract the devoted. When those songs ended, inspirational music would replace the soft demands. Often this music, sung by favorite contemporary singers, would express an emotion and beauty that cut right into my heart.

"The oven of my chest and heart…" began one singer, as he describes his secret love for a country free of oppression. It was a thinly veiled political statement, hidden in the words of a song.

Invariably, these songs would cause Aghajune to burst into song with long, impassioned, soulful songs of his own that seemed antithetical to the stern patriarch his children were accustomed to. He would sing loudly and with enormous gusto, his voice a clear and soothing tenor. And when he had finished, he would smile self-consciously and say, "I am finished," and cross his arms as if to signal *The End*.

My brother-in-law fancied himself a poet and would then break into verse. This, of course, prompted yet more singing and competitive poetry. We would laugh and eat and drink tea. And the sound of the music emanating from the minaret would fade into the night sky.

The Revolutionary Guards stationed near our home also liked to play music during the day. Inspirational marching tunes and contemporary revolutionary music were favorites. I tolerated this, to a point.

They would blare out the same songs over and over again throughout the day. These were songs intended to inspire, and they filled the neighborhood. Ignorant of the origins of some of the songs but drawn to the melody, the guards would play songs by John Phillip Sousa. They even began playing the US Marine Corps hymn. I actually considered dropping by one day to point out the irony. But after some thought, I figured I'd just let them continue to embarrass themselves. One day the song simply dropped off the top-ten play list.

I had to pass by those guards daily. Everyone on our street did. I would avoid meeting their gaze as I turned the corner to walk up the hill to our front door. These were the days before the Revolutionary

Guards were molded into an elite fighting force. The guards were recruiting and consolidating power. By and large during this period they were a bunch of kids in brand-new uniforms with AK-47s who stood behind their gates, periodically making comments to me.

When I first arrived in Iran, I had no idea what they were saying. As a result, I paid little attention to them. Over time, however, my status as a curiosity in their minds became known to me.

"Here comes that woman from the land of the great Satan," one would remark astonished. "Look at how big she is." The others would nod in agreement.

One—a young boy, perhaps from a distant, isolated village—would say, "They grow them big there."

I would walk down the streets of Tehran—a six-foot, blue-eyed American woman in clogs—and invariably be accosted by children. They were both curious and terrified. I got a lot of that, "they grow them big in the land of the great Satan," in those years. I would smile, point at them, and make that sound they made on Star Trek when the crew was beamed up to the mother ship. The kids would run from me in terror.

Upper-middle-class, professional, educated Iranians had, of course, many experiences with foreigners and were thus not so impressed with me. I was anything but stylish and was looked upon with something close to pity at family outings.

It was, however, the man on the street—the shopkeeper's young assistant, the child hanging around the stall at the open-air bazaar—who really interested me, and I in turn interested them. I discovered early on there was a premium price I paid as a foreigner. This became wholly apparent during my first foray into shopping unassisted, I came back dismayed. I had been given the worst produce and had paid twice the price for it.

The markets in Iran were greatly impacted by the embargo and war shortages. Again, because Iran's prior agricultural self-sufficiency was essentially destroyed by the Shah, foods were largely imported and seasonal. In the Winter months, oranges filled the carts. Vendors stood ready to sell. But the shopper was not allowed to touch the fruit. Pointing at an orange, or demanding a certain piece of fruit was ignored. One simply asked for a kilo or so of oranges, and the vendor, extending his hand to its full width, deftly grabbed four at a time and placed them in a paper bag.

It was a sleight of hand trick, I discovered. Much effort is expended by the vendors in arranging the fruits and vegetables in such a manner as to make sure each customer gets one really good piece and three pieces of lesser quality. It was always disconcerting for me as I poured the contents of my shopping spree out on the kitchen table. My sister-in-law, Parvaneh, assured me that this happened to everyone; that I had not been singled out because I was a foreigner. She was, of course, lying to me to spare my feelings. I was "a mark".

However, the aggressive, seasoned shopper (a.k.a. my mother-in-law), having spent decades suffering through this strange, imposed, equal-opportunity crap selling, would simply yell loudly until she browbeat the vendor into giving her what she wanted.

I noticed other women cajoling, criticizing, and gesturing as well. I, however, appeared to have been the dream customer. I made a scene with mere presence, so I really didn't feel like pushing my luck.

"They keep giving me crap" I complained loudly to Hadj.

It was already dark, and Hadj ascended the two steps leading from the heavy metal front door to the foyer. He held a small paper bag, which he handed to me.

"Butter and milk," he declared. "They have them for sale near work."

"I can't seem to get good stuff. They see me and they give me crap," I whined.

"It's the system, Lisa*khanuum*" he stated matter-of-factly. "It's how they work".

"Well, we need our own system."

In an attempt to circumvent the system, Hadj would walk behind me as I meandered through the stalls, noting what was available. If I wanted something, I would stop, talk for a minute with the vendor, then move on empty-handed. He would then approach after I had left and buy something. It worked relatively well for a while. But, I was an unusual sight in our *Tajrish* neighborhood and easily picked out of a crowd. Eventually, the merchants caught on and even Hadj got taken at the produce stall. I just began to see it as a cost of doing business as a tall foreigner in Iran and let it go.

Had the offerings of the open market been plentiful and my choices really impacted, I am sure I would have been far more infuriated by my treatment. But inflation and lack of inventory impacted the availability of produce. Over time, it was not uncommon to have a single available choice. One year, cauliflower was the only readily available vegetable in season. I became a pro at cooking cauliflower a thousand different ways.

Further, the markets uptown in our neighborhood were not as well stocked as the ones in the south of the city. The government had made a conscious decision to make sure it's power base among the working poor reaped all of the benefits of the revolution, while punishing the wealthier by creating shortages. Our local supermarket contained an inordinate number of containers of Quaker Oats, a delicacy I am not entirely sure Iranian's enjoyed eating. They lined the shelves, with that cheerful Quaker man looking ho on anyone who approached. Had it not been so demons tough economic times, it would have been comical.

And so, as Hadj worked in the south where the regime placated its supporters by making sure their markets were stocked, he took to grocery shopping near the factory before starting his hour commute home.

CHAPTER 13
TRADITIONS AND TIME MANAGEMENT

Persian New Year falls on the first day of spring each year. During a period of two weeks, homes are visited and gifts are brought. The homeowner must be vigilant, as a guest may arrive at any moment. Tea should be brewed and served, cakes cut, flowers placed in a vase in the pristine sitting room. A small mountain of fruit had to be at the ready to be served.

Initially I thought it was a little stressful, but I came to appreciate the tradition. The Persian New Year is not a Muslim event. It is a holiday that celebrates the first day of spring, rebirth, and renewal. It is a time to cast off the old and embrace the new. As you might well imagine, the conservative clerics were not particularly thrilled with this *casting-off* concept. They tried to ban all the festivities. And failed.

On the Tuesday before the New Year—*Chahar Shanbeh Soori*—old and young alike congregate on the streets to jump over burning bushes. As they leap across the burning tumbleweed, they yell out: "*Zardi-e man az to; sorkhi-e to az man.*" The literal translation is "My yellow is yours; your red is mine." This is a purification rite that, loosely translated, means that you want the fire to take your pallor, sickness and problems away and in turn give you redness, warmth and energy. While the holiday has its roots in Zoroastrianism,, it is truly a cultural event for Iranians—and an important one at that.

During the weeks before the New Year, new clothes are bought or made, and houses are cleaned from top to bottom for the annual spring cleaning. Families prepare for the onslaught of visitors making the rounds. The *sofreh*, or tablecloth, is covered with seven items, each with a name starting with an *S* sound. They symbolize fertility, birth and rebirth. Photos of the departed are carefully placed among these symbols.

And then of course there is the food—massive amounts of fragrant, rich and delectable food. Turmeric, saffron, garlic, cinnamon, herbs, fruits and meats all combined—a delicious medley combining the savory with the sweet; rice, fragrant and formed into large cakes, with the crunchy *tadeek* (crust) exposed for the lucky to enjoy.

These are the textures and the flavors of the Persian New Year. Food and family, family and food. This is my Iran. This is what I know and these were the people who welcomed me with generosity into their families.

When invited to dine at the home of an Iranian family, the table is covered with food. It is considered impolite to offer a single entrée, and you will never find salad as a main course. Rice figures prominently. Not unlike other rice-centered cultures, there are many names for it: raw rice is *barrenge*; sticky rice is *cat teh*; fluffy Basmati rice is *pollo*. The rice is cooked in a rice maker until the crispy brown bottom of the pan has produced the coveted crust. Then, once that is done, the entire pot is flipped onto a serving dish and served in a cake-like form. Sometimes saffron with yogurt is added to the rice, creating *ta chin*. It's yellow and tangy and wonderful.

Red currants called *zer reshk* create a tangy, fruity texture in white rice. Often these currants are added to the yellow rice. The effect is beautiful. And then there is the *khoresh*—stews made with lamb, beef, or chicken, always paired with some fruit (beef and plums, lamb and dried lemons), and eggplants or chickpeas ladled over a huge mound of rice and accompanied by homemade yogurt.

There are not enough glowing adjectives to describe how good this food is. There was very little I avoided eating. I was offered once, and declined, a dish called *cal o pah cheh*, which roughly translates into "the head, the foot, and everything else." I am not sure if she was kidding or not, but my sister-in-law told me the eyeballs float to the surface. I had no desire to eat an eyeball. I know somewhere in the Middle East someone is in foodie heaven eating his or her weight in eyeballs. It will never be me.

I did enjoy, however, a dish called *khaleem*, made with turkey. To me this dish symbolized all that was frustrating about living in the developing world. It offered a stark insight into the very real differences between the Iranian way and the American way. *Khaleem* is a breakfast food made by cooking turkey for an eternity, mixing in grains, smashing it all up, and then repeating the whole process again and again until you end up with a food the consistency of oatmeal. It actually tastes like oatmeal and is eaten with sugar just like oatmeal. It is the color of oatmeal. It is served on the streets to workmen needing something hearty before starting the day. It requires hours and hours and hours to prepare.

After she explained the entire process to me in great detail, I asked my sister-in-law why she didn't simply blend all the stuff together and then cook it. I am not sure if she was kidding, but her response was, "No wonder you Americans are so powerful! I had never thought of doing that!"

"You're kidding?" I thought to myself.

I dare suggest that Americans tend to be in a hurry. We often crave immediate gratification. We love to have good food made easily. Iranians are not in a hurry. Everything takes, literally and figuratively, forever to get done. The rice—well, you know—one must pull out the rocks. The vegetables have to be sanitized. And that is just the start.

Tomato paste is the ingredient that forms the base of many Persian stews and is created by the time-consuming process of cooking down fresh, crushed, and strained tomatoes. It takes hours. Many Europeans take the time to make their own tomato sauces. Americans, however, tend to prefer opening cans. It is simply a matter of time management.

We do not easily give up our ways when we live in foreign lands. We can respect, conform, learn and mimic, but we will always fall back on what we know. I would always be the American bride. I knew this. I attempted to fit in as best I could, but there would always be that thin barrier between me and the other women.

When I first arrived with Hadj and our ten suitcases, my initial response to the culture shock was to attempt to be "one" with my fellow Iranians. I would do as they do, I vowed. I would dress as they dress. I would live as they lived. But my California upbringing was deeply ingrained in me and, as I came to accept, there really is an American way. I resisted. I tried to bury my American way as best I could. To be honest, I was not entirely sure what the American way was. But, a wholesale rejection of my American upbringing would be, as my grandmother would say, just "throwing the baby out with the bathwater."

I would observe my mother-in-law going through the tedious processes of preparing a meal and think to myself that there must be a more efficient way for her to accomplish the same result in half the time. I needed to mask my derision while watching her do something so labor – and time-intensive—something I believed could be far more efficiently done with the aid of a blender.

Trying to be both culturally sensitive and cheerfully helpful, I would approach her with a myriad of time-saving suggestions. She would hear me out and, looking almost ashamed, agree that, yes, my way was better…and then continue doing what she was doing. It took me quite a while to understand the hold that *her way* had on her. It was just as powerful as mine. Her techniques and methods gave her comfort, just as mine did for me. It was familiar and good, as was mine. But for me, the pace could be excruciating. Just as Hadj had learned when sourcing parts for this factory, *fardah* (tomorrow) could mean anytime between tomorrow and the end of time as we know it. For someone used to going and doing and being and moving and shaking, spending a lazy afternoon with a large aluminum tray on my lap cleaning the small pebbles out of the rice seemed like a frustratingly unnecessary waste of time.

CHAPTER 14
FRIEND OF THE REVOLUTION

Shortly after my return to Iran, I insinuated myself into the favor of Abolhassan Sadegh, the Minister of National Guidance. A former military man trained in the US, he had been appointed to the position by then-president Abolhassan Bani Sadr, a moderate-centrist. At the time, among his other official duties, he was responsible for issuing press passes to foreign journalists. He also organized press tours and other events, hoping the foreign media would focus on the positives following the revolution.

He was a short, balding man with a friendly, earnest face. Hadj's eldest sister worked as a translator for him, and she had introduced us. She and her colleagues would translate current articles from US and other foreign magazines and prepare weekly press briefings for government officials. I met Sadegh one day, and, after spending a half hour getting through the mandatory small talk, he asked me if I would help him deal with the foreign press.

Sadegh was very much out of his depth at the ministry. While he had been a great supporter of Khomeini, he was not particularly well-read and certainly not very knowledgeable about international current events. He simply had a deep hatred for the Shah's regime. As if to win me over to his thinking, he produced a scrapbook, which contained graphic and disturbing photographs of men who had been tortured and killed by the Shah's secret police. I assured him he was speaking with a sympathizer. I was already on his side.

"I don't know much about the foreign press," he confided. "Is *US News & World Report* a real magazine?"

"It is," I replied. "You should let them all come in." This I boldly volunteered without being asked.

"Could you do something for me?" he asked, somewhat sheepishly. "Could you go out into the office and speak with the reporters? Find out where they are from and what they want."

"Sure," I replied. "I can do that."

The outer office was filled with men with cameras and vests holding pens and other journalistic accessories. There were others who looked anxious and confused. I assumed they were reporters or journalists. Most of the men appeared to be Americans or Europeans, with a sprinkling of Asians.

I approached a man carrying a large camera slung over his shoulder. The camera was decorated with a sticker declaring it to be from an Asian news agency. The cameraman, however, was not Asian, which piqued my curiosity.

"Where are you really from?" I asked him in a straightforward manner, pointing at his sticker. "You're not from this agency, are you?"

"No," he laughed, peeling back the label on the camera gently to reveal the ABC News logo underneath.

"Oh, ABC News. Does Sadegh know?" I asked.

"Hope not," he replied.

I turned and reentered Sadegh's private office.

"They are all good. Give them all credentials," I said matter-of-factly.

He issued credentials to everyone standing outside his door that day.

I made a number of trips to see Sadegh in his office.

"This is for you," he announced, clearly pleased with himself, as he handed me a very official-looking lapel pass. "It says you are a friend of the revolution," he explained. "You can go anywhere now."

I realized that I was now in the charmed position of being able to see what the international press was seeing, while having access to buildings and press conferences, prisons and palaces I would otherwise not be able to see. More importantly, I now belonged there. I was, after all, a "Friend of the Revolution." It said so on my badge.

And thus armed with something "official," I stood with a group of male journalists, waiting for the minibus that would transport us to various sites throughout the city. There were less than ten of us. Some of the men seemed to know each other. As the lone woman, dressed in my head scarf and overcoat, no one bothered to speak with me. For my part, I felt a little like a fraud attending the tour under false pretenses with my made-up pass. I opted to keep to myself and observe.

Driving deep into the center of Tehran, our minibus pulled up to a large stark and imposing prison. It was the Central Prison and, true to its name, near the center of Tehran. It was unremarkable in its appearance; it looked like a gray windowless structure imposing itself among the small shops and streets that surrounded it.

This place was one of many where torture chambers were created. Metal chairs with steel cuffs were placed on concrete platforms stationed in the middle of shiny black-tiled rooms.

"The black tile reflected the strobe lights," our guide explained. He was a youngish man and the room clearly disturbed him as much as it did me. The strobe lights were intended to disorient and distort reality. They caused fear, he explained. Strapped into a chair, eyes forced open, the strobe lights would assault the prisoner until he confessed or passed out.

"These are the tools they used," he said, pointing to the walls containing chains and steel pliers and other devices I had gladly never seen before.

The floors were concrete and stained. "It is blood," he said. I didn't even need to ask.

I knew that I was being taken on a propaganda tour calculated to discredit and indict the Shah's regime. The sight of actual torture rooms and devices sickened me. I had, for the past few years, spent much time telling people in California about the Shah's torture. I knew at that time I spoke the truth. I had, however, never expected to see the actual scenes of torture for myself.

We filed back into the bus and headed uptown to the Shah's "screwing palace." It was smallish for a palace and had been given that inglorious title as it was where the Shah had chosen to entertain his various mistresses.

The grounds of the palace were made up of vast, gently sloping lawns on which various large sculptures were found. Statues, both classical and contemporary, were scattered among the roses.

We strolled the gardens on gravel pathways, wandering through the art, when I spotted it: a thumbs-up statue, at least six feet high and over eight feet long. A plaque adorned its granite pedestal: "To the Iranian people from the American people."

"Oh my God," I exclaimed to no one in particular as the offending sculpture came into view. "Is this some sort of joke?"

In Iran, the thumbs-up gesture is the equivalent of a middle-finger salute. The employees of the US Department of State, diplomats of one of the most powerful and populous countries in the world, had apparently not bothered to do any cultural research before presenting the Iranian people with this large metal symbol of obscenity.

In contrast, the Walt Disney Company spent millions of dollars researching, testing, confirming, and rejecting hand signals for their amusement parks. They wanted to make sure that they did not offend anyone by making a cultural faux pas. For instance, Disney cast members gesture people to move along in lines by using their index and middle finger placed together and horizontally, slightly bent toward the palm, and in a soft and gentle swinging motion. They had discovered this gesture offends no one.

Unfortunately, by failing to do proper homework, the US Department of State offended an entire nation.

I turned to the small group of journalists and explained to them the inadvertent blunder. No one seemed particularly interested.

"Do you understand what's wrong with this?" I asked again. "Don't you see the irony?" I implored.

Unmoved, the group walked away.

CHAPTER 15
SMALL REBELLIONS

In January 1980, Bani Sadr was elected as Iran's first president. Politically a "centrist," Bani Sadr walked the tightrope between Khomeini's fundamentalism and his secular past. Bani Sadr, unlike others in power at that time, was not a cleric. He was an engineer who would give long, often excruciatingly detailed speeches, which contrasted sharply with the simple, repetitive message that characterized Khomeini's style of speech.

At the time, Iran's Parliament still boasted members with various political party affiliations. But Khomeini's party held firmly onto its majority.

The bloom of hope had still not faded. People still had high hopes of a more open society and those in my social group saw the election of a "civilian" as a good sign.

"This man loves the sound of his own voice," Hadj would observe, as Bani Sadr appeared to drone on and on during one of his innumerable televised speeches.

"Khomeini comes up with a central message, then slowly and simply repeats it, over and over and over again," he noted. "He is appealing to the most naïve peasant. Bani Sadr is speaking to intellectuals."

Bani Sadr did not have an organized political party behind him. He ran his election simply as a candidate. His lack of a political power base would come to haunt him in the end and weaken his impact, but at the time his election was welcomed as a sign that Iran's Islamic Republic would be a moderate, socially progressive one.

Between March and May of 1980, the Iranian parliament was experiencing loud and forceful debates over the contents of Iran's "new" constitution. Forces seeking to consolidate the rule of Khomeini wanted to include a provision that created the role of *velayat-e faqi* or supreme leader. While the first draft of Iran's new constitution omitted reference to this, ultimately it was included and, no surprise, Khomeini was installed in the post. The role of the supreme leader was to ensure the dominance of Shi'a Islam over all aspects of Iranian politics. Every parliamentary action had to be reviewed and approved as to conforming with the supreme leader's interpretation of Islam. The net effect was to effectively muzzle any authentic opposition.

This was a time in Iran of the Islamization of schools and universities. Thousands of teachers and professors lost their jobs. Khomeini declared a new "cultural revolution" to replace the "old" learning with Islam-centric teachings.

By August of 1980, Amnesty International was appealing to Iran to stop executing dissenters and pro-Shah figures in the wake of at least one thousand executions.

Our initial enthusiasm and hope for real change began to disintegrate. In the face of ever-increasing repression, new forces of open opposition began to slowly emerge. Fear and uncertainty bred rebellion in subtle and often amusing ways. It was not uncommon to be driving down a main thoroughfare and notice that someone had annotated the official murals declaring "Long live Rafsanjani, Long Live Beheshti, Long Live Khomeini" (three notorious and powerful clerics) with the subtle caption: "Society for the prevention of cruelty to animals." This was rebel humor at its best.

Not to be outdone, we did our part, too. We had pool parties during the holy month of Ramadan, during which devout practicing Muslims refrain from eating or submerging their heads underwater from sunrise to sundown. Our parties featured much food and a great deal of noisy pool games. This would have been unremarkable, except for the fact that we lived across the street from one of the entrances to Saad Abad palace, which had been taken over by Revolutionary Guards, who were watching us constantly. My nephew, Ali, would run from his house next door in his bathing suit with empty trays that had previously carried food. Sometimes, just to avoid the risk of detection, he and his sister Nazanin would simply jump over the fence from their garden into ours below. We were all young and fearless, and would have a great old time thumbing our noses at the regime's strict mandates.

In the face of the wave of new conservative Islamic regulations, we tried to maintain as much normalcy as we could. Whenever we had parties, I would serve the nonreligious relatives screwdrivers made with our precious bootleg vodka distilled by our Armenian neighbor in his bathtub. Conservative and restriction-adherent Muslims would get just plain ol' OJ. I always suspected that the teetotalers knew what we were up to but politely declined to comment.

Iranian television at the time had little programming beyond propaganda unartfully disguised as the news. We did, however, have *Zorro*. To the regime, this program was revolution at its best: the small guy fighting the evil colonial power. Every Friday afternoon at two thirty, the city stopped to watch *Zorro*. I suspected that Zorro and his fight against the Spanish colonialists, with their decadent ruling class, resonated strongly. For me, it was nostalgic. It was the *Zorro* of my youth, circa 1960—dubbed. It was heaven for half an hour each week.

As the Islamic noose tightened, rule-breaking became a part of our daily lives. We had access to forbidden foreign videos, and periodically I would go with my sister-in-law to watch a movie in English. We would dress up (well, she would—I was not that chic) and drive to the home of a woman friend, where we would sit drinking tea from very expensive china in a very ornate room and watch an American B movie. I was brought along not only to enjoy the show, but also to explain some of the nuances and slang in the films. It was always a great outing, particularly as these women went all out on the desserts.

Early on in the revolution, women were expected to cover themselves, but the national dress for women—the head scarf and overcoat, *roo sari* or *roo pusht*—had not yet been mandated. The ratification of the new, Islamic Constitution cemented the mandatory *hajib* as the strictly required national dress for women.

At first, I wore the scarf casually draped over my head, my bangs hanging out, loosely flung behind my head. I wore my personal version of the overcoat, a longish cotton tunic jacket I'd bought at Macy's. I wore jeans and—to the amusement of just about everyone—I wore clogs.

I had always had short hair. In 1972, after having seen the movie *Klute*, I cut my hair into that trendy shag that Jane Fonda sported. I was the only girl in my high-school yearbook with short hair. In 1978, when I first went to Iran, my hair was mid-length and I had one of those home perms intended to give lifeless straight hair some curl and body. By 1980, when head scarves were mandatory and I started wearing a headscarf most days in the heat and the cold, I decided to cut all my hair off. Standing in our bathroom with scissors in hand, I gave myself a girlie version of a crew cut.

Further, I decided to stop wearing the synthetic scarf and switched to a cotton dishrag. I did this for two reasons: Firstly, the rags were made of soft white cotton, they were natural, they breathed, and I loved them. And secondly, I just got a kick out of people stopping me with a perplexed look and saying, "*Khanuum*, you know that is a dishrag, right?"

I would smile knowingly and say, "I do." I felt like such a rebel.

Before moving to Iran, I had heard so much about Iranian politics, but very little about the culture. Through osmosis, however, I had learned some basics—simple things—from Iranian friends. They would casually mention one thing or the other. But the most alien concept to me was the mystery of *tarof*.

Tarof as a concept is truly almost absurd to most Westerners. It is a cultural phenomenon that underscores the real graciousness I've found most Iranians sincerely demonstrate. It is a give-and-take scenario that goes like this: When offered something—an item, a service—you are *required* first to say, "Oh, no, thank you, I couldn't." The person making the offer, thus rebuffed, counters by insisting, "No, you must take it." Once again you refuse, protesting, "I couldn't possibly." This goes on for a while, until eventually the recipient concedes. It is a dance, a game that defines how people interact. It is almost mandatory and both a confusing and confounding cultural staple facing most American visitors. Once learned, however, it can be rather useful.

But during my maiden voyage to Iran in 1978, as an uninitiated visitor, I had yet to learn the nuance of *tarof*. It simultaneously confused and infuriated me. No meant no, right? Or did no mean maybe if you force me to take it? Who could tell?

In the hopes of limiting the number of people I accidentally insulted on any given day, I just made sure to surrender to any offer of food or drink, smiling and vigorously nodding my head with inappropriately demonstrative abandon.

My knowledge of *tarof* was helpful after coming back to the United States in 1982. I was given a job with a feminist women's health clinic, which shortly after my arrival announced the formation of its new sperm bank. The local press carried the headline along the lines of *Women Make Babies Without Men*, which of course was both ridiculous and inaccurate. The director of the clinic and I would fly around the country doing television and radio interviews about the work of the clinic and the sperm bank.

On one such trip, we found ourselves flying into the airport in Burbank, near Los Angeles, to be guests on *The Merv Griffin Show*. We had very, very limited funds in those days, and the show's producers told us to take a cab. They had promised to reimburse us. However, we had less than two dollars between us.

We hailed a cab at the airport, and to my delight our driver and his passenger-helper were both Iranian. When my colleague told them we were going to the Merv Griffin Studios—the driver turned to his friend and said in Farsi, "Do you know how to get there?"

His companion replied, "I have no idea. Just drive around. They are strangers. They won't know. We will find it."

Cheerfully they drove around town and into an area that they suspected contained the studio. Chatting casually, they repeatedly joked about taking us for what they hoped was an expensive ride.

Finally, after a half hour or so of this nonsense, we happened upon the studio.

"Have you no shame?" I asked in Farsi as we got out. "I know you didn't know where to go. I understood you."

He looked at me as if I had grown a second head. A tall, blue-eyed American woman speaking Farsi was more than he and his cohort could fathom. Both of them then fell all over themselves complimenting me on my Farsi, telling me how happy they were to have driven an American friend, and so forth. It was all for show.

After suffering through a minute or so of this, and because we needed to get a move on, I finally asked him "How much?"

"Oh, *Khanuum*," he replied, hand to chest, head tilting forward slightly, looking somewhat contrite. "Oh, *Khanuum*. please, it is nothing."

"Good," I said and walked away, hearing only the diminishing sounds of him yelling after us for money.

CHAPTER 16
TEACHING
"ESCAPE ENGLISH"

By late 1980, with his factory operating in full swing, Hadj informed me that we would start an English-language institute in a five-story office building also owned by Hadj's father in midtown Tehran. The building had been largely vacant and Aghajune feared the regime would try to confiscate it by declaring it abandoned, as they had been doing to other landlords at that time.

For our outwardly purposes, it was the perfect set-up and we were of course happy to assist Aghajune in any way. We used one of the available suites of offices—a large room divided into several smaller classrooms. We bought a couple of used blackboards and a mimeograph machine, gave ourselves what we thought was an official-sounding name, and threw open our doors. Our claim to fame was that all of our teachers were native speakers.

My days at Iranzamin School with my third graders ended at two o'clock, and as shops and businesses closed each day for a siesta between noon and four o'clock, I would commute to our new school daily to teach my eager students practical English.

These were the times when young middle-class families, who had been so hopeful and enthusiastic about social change following the downfall of the Shah, began to experience the tightening repression and social conservatism that now gripped the country. Our students would attend classes religiously for a few weeks, pay up, and then disappear. We began to refer to our classes, among ourselves, as "escape English" hoping that we had provided our students with enough tools to help them relocate outside Iran.

The tide of religious fanaticism had swept the nation, fueled by the war with Iraq, which began in September 1980. The war fostered an intense nationalism among the proud Iranians who believed that Saddam Hussein was America's puppet. In the eyes of many, the war with Iraq was in no small way a proxy war between an isolated and embargoed Iran and the powerful America. Moreover, the majority of Muslims in Iraq were Sunni and were presented as rivals to the Iranian Shi'a majority.

The war was an excellent propaganda tool that heightened the hold of the fundamentalists, who used Friday prayer to further their political ambitions and fan the flames of ultraorthodox patriotism among their followers. The constant struggle between those loyal to President Bani Sadr and the forces of conservative fundamentalism had intensified. Assassinations of major religious leaders and bombings of buildings and offices rocked Tehran.

Conversely, among a small section of the population, a developing populist movement in opposition to the conservative faction of the regime began to develop. There were rumblings of discontent and the authorities were coming down hard and fast on the opposition. The international economic isolation that resulted from the seizure of the US embassy created a stranglehold on the economy. Jobs for the educated were becoming difficult to find. Jobs for the secular or more liberal professional were nearly nonexistent. As a result, college-educated, middle-class professionals began to leave the country in droves, heartbroken and penniless. Their dreams of a new, free Iran had been crushed.

Our students were taught how to write a résumé and how to conduct themselves in job interviews. We showed them how to fill out immigration forms. We spent a great deal of time explaining how to ask for and receive directions, which, if you have ever tried to learn this in a new language, is extremely difficult. We wrote letters for them to show prospective employers their proficiency in English.

We had a Gestetner mimeograph machine, the predecessor of the photocopier. You would write on a special paper to create lines on the page that would allow ink to pass through. The paper was placed on a drum, which would go around and around as the ink was applied, and print a copy. It was fast, cheap, and a little messy. It was a process prohibited by the regime—except, of course, if you had a school. The government did not want ordinary citizens to have access to a machine that could mass produce leaflets, booklets and other writings that might be used for political purposes. Which, of course, was exactly why we started our school and bought the machine in the first place.

Each night, someone would enter the building and spend hours printing fliers that mysteriously appeared in the hands of protesters, on walls, and taped to trees. Just as mysteriously, they would leave without a trace. It was a great system. We had no idea who they were. We just knew they had been there.

Our teachers were former lawyers, writers, and housewives from various parts of the United States. We were all the wives of Iranian student activists or activist sympathizers who were drawn together by a hope for a better future for our adopted country. In varying degrees, they were also, as was I, former political and social activists in their home states. And, not unlike Hadj's factory, our school was slated to be used as a cover for his comrades in some way. We would, of course, also teach people how to navigate in English.

For our small part as supporters of Hadj's political movement, we teachers would meet regularly with "a contact" assigned to help us analyze international political events to put the appropriate leftist spin on events and write articles about these events to be later published in papers we could not even read. The rule at the time was clear: We could only know one person involved in the underground political movement. The thinking was simply that if arrested, we could only give up one name. We knew better than to ask him his name or attempt to solicit any information about him. He was our man and he was assigned to help us. That is really all we needed to know.

We would sit for hours on the floor of one of our classrooms, hotly debating the significance of an event that had occurred somewhere in the world, four American women arguing with each other about some current event that took place months before in another country. I believe it made us feel useful. Our "guy" would sit silently and take notes. I doubt that he had ever in his life had to deal with that many American women, particularly our brand of vocal and pushy left-leaning types. We took ourselves so very, very seriously. Little did we know, but would come to find out, the Khomeini regime did as well.

The turmoil of the times gave way to protests and riots by citizens demanding the regime implement social and economic changes. The People's Mujahideen, a left-leaning organization that violently opposed the fundamentalist government, was growing in strength. Founded by radicalized, leftist Muslim college students in the 1960s, the People's Mujahideen found itself the constant target of the fundamentalist right wing of the post-revolutionary forces who attacked their meetings, bookstores, and members mercilessly. They held protest demonstrations that erupted in violence when armed government forces attacked.

The location of our school was such that during the riots we could see the protesters running from the armed thugs down the streets. Our building was on a corner, allowing us to view a central *meydoon* to our left and the streets that bisected it. We were on the fifth floor and high enough to have a relatively unobstructed view. Massive demonstrations and strikes were being held regularly.

Protesters would amass in or around the square, holding home-made signs and banners and chanting their demands loudly. With fists punching the air, they would move almost in unison, a pulsating human block of anger and energy.

Uniformed Revolutionary Guards and other plain-clothed assorted enforcers would follow on motorbikes, speeding through the crowds, over sidewalks, and between parked cars. When the mass would reach an open square and at the height of their vocal protests, some unseen signal would be given and the guards would attack and disburse the crowds.

The protesters, seeking to divert the attentions of the guards and guard supporters, would set car tires on fire, filling the sky with the acrid smell of burning rubber.

I would lean out the window, mesmerized by the clashes below.

"Lisa*Khanuum*," Hadj would admonish. "They can shoot up too. Get your head in here!" he would command.

It was during these demonstrations that I stumbled upon the hidden power of the *chador* and its striking alternative use. *Chador* means tent. It is a dark, often black, cape that a devout woman uses to cover her head and body. Wrapping it over her head and clasping it in her teeth freed up the woman's hands so that she could carry her child or a basket.

There is some disagreement regarding the true origins of that garment; some scholars believe the *chador* originated as a method of shielding the wives of the wealthy from view. Rich feudal landlords would transport their numerous wives on platforms built on the backs of camels. On top of the platform was a tent, safeguarding the wives from prying eyes. The lesser feudal lords could not afford all the paraphernalia. Possessing neither the platform, nor the camel, they created their own moving tents, in the form of the *chador*. Thus, the *chador* was born.

By 1980 the new Islamic regime was attempting to impose its view of a moral dress code on all women. The *hijab*, or appropriate, traditional dress for Muslim women, was different from the *chador*. It was comprised of a head covering and a below-the-knee-length overcoat, both usually navy blue or beige. The *chador* had no clasp or pocket and was unwieldy and difficult to manage.

Female protesters would often use the *chador* to escape capture by the authorities. Leaning out of our building's open windows, I peered down on a crowd of disbursing protesters. I saw two women—covered in that black garment—run down the street away from the gun-toting Revolutionary Guards. Quickly they would turn the corner of our street and let their *chadors* slip silently into the open sewer that bordered the sidewalk. Underneath the shroud they wore regular head scarves and were dressed as young college students, or uptown housewives. Turning abruptly, they would walk back around the corner toward their pursuers, who had no idea that these two well-dressed women were the same two they had been chasing moments before. It worked for them. I was fascinated.

The tightening grip of the hardliners had given birth to both mass demonstrations and small, personal acts of rebellion. The sight of those two women using what at that time came to be seen as a symbol of devotion to the ruling faction as a tool of their rebellion remained etched in my mind as yet another display of Iranian rebel creativity.

CHAPTER 17

I was there on April 25, 1980, during the Tabas incident, or Operation Eagle Claw. Two American helicopters tragically crashed during an unexpected storm in the barren desert outside of Tehran near the city of Tabas. The pilots died and the regime, horrifically, displayed their charred remains on television.

The stated mission was to surreptitiously enter Tehran and free the hostages. Apparently, the authorities thought the hostages were still being held at the embassy compound. This was not the case as we now know.

The hardliners and authorities, of course, used this tragedy to conduct yet another media propaganda campaign. The nightly news, controlled by the fundamentalists, showed us footage of smiling Revolutionary Guards desecrating the burned bodies of the fallen soldiers. It was horrific and yet strangely routine. It was not unusual for the news to broadcast film of bodies. Blood and gore, death and destruction were daily topics in Iran. The American soldiers were just another example, and the regime revealed to all the extent of its barbarism.

Hard as it may be to believe, we "knew" they were coming. We knew something was up, and we knew it related to the hostages.

On the evening of Friday, April 25, 1980, Hadj and I went to a small dinner party at an apartment located down a short alley, with a balcony that directly overlooked the US embassy. We had no idea at that time that the helicopters had crashed as the news of the tragedy had not yet been broadcast. It was, we joked, a watch-what-happens-now party.

On that day, uncharacteristically, the streets of Tehran were lousy with soldiers. Even more strangely, one by one the enormous 20-millimeter anti-aircraft guns that were placed on the mountain ridge surrounding the city to the north, were towed through Tehran, down the main boulevard to the south of the city for "servicing." The net effect of all of this was of course that the city stood unprotected from any assault from the air.

And then of course there was the embassy itself. The stadium lights were on, clearly illuminating the football field. The lights in the buildings were on. The lights outside the building were on. The US embassy was lit up like a Christmas tree.

Rumor had spread through Tehran that a US helicopter would fly over the city, spraying sleeping gas to disarm the guards in the embassy. They went on to say that once the residents of Tehran were safely disposed of, airmen would land in the embassy compound and free the hostages. We had all watched far too many action movies. But stranger things have happened in the world of special ops, and I wasn't going to completely dismiss the rumor.

We also heard that the military radio signals were jammed that night—pro-American military saboteurs were interfering with communications to disrupt the ability of the Revolutionary Guard to respond. That was perfectly plausible, as the military supported Bani Sadr.

On the day before the crash, strangely and inexplicably, the soldiers (not the Revolutionary Guards) who manned the anti-aircraft guns close to our house, were put on leave. In fact, most of the military was on leave that day. It is important here to note that at that time, and within the context of the continuing struggle between the Right and the Center, led by Bani Sadr, the military supported the president. Iranian military officers of rank were routinely trained by US advisers or in the United States itself. The Iranian military immediately after the revolution was composed of substantially the same forces as before. Only the most offending generals were executed or escaped into exile if they were lucky. I dare suggest that it would not be outside the realm of possibility for this rumor to have been based in truth.

And so, we went to the party and waited. We stood there in the dark, all of us on the balcony, peering over and into the embassy compound. It was a fun event, but alas, no sleeping gas, no helicopter, no US Special Forces. We left somewhat dejected. The next day we heard the news.

By the time the hostages were released, the world knew they had been separated and taken to remote locations. The embassy itself was a red herring. The mission to free them would have been a huge failure. Did the authorities know they were coming and lit the embassy to trick them? Was it all a set-up from the start? Who knows? It failed, and diplomacy worked.

CHAPTER 18

We began to get visitors who were self-described delegates from various organizations in the United States. Some of our visitors came in an official capacity representing their groups. They had very specific agendas; plans to meet and investigate. They spent several weeks touring the country and taking pictures. Invariably they would return to the United States, hold conferences, publish books and do a pretty good job discussing the current politics in Iran with the general public.

They would often, however, come with idealistic notions and expectations. They didn't seem to grasp the fact that we just couldn't go out and hawk revolutionary newspapers on street corners as they did back home. They brought with them dozens of copies of such newspapers, ostensibly as gifts to be passed around. The papers would end up with me, and I would find myself burning them in the dead of night in our backyard, a tarp covering up the light of the fire and causing me to choke on the smoke that wafted up into the night sky.

In late May 1980, we hosted an American woman who came to Iran to see the sights and experience the revolution firsthand. She was a prominent member of a feminist group that had given much support to the Iranian Students Association over the years. She had a deep and thorough understanding of Iranian political history and a fearless desire to see the revolution up close.

During my years of political activism in California, I had met many American women who identified themselves as feminists. This particular label distinguished them from other women whose political interests were more broadly general issues of social justice and change.

I had worked with them on many occasions, and I was familiar with the ideology, the scope of which I sometimes found too narrow as I fancied myself more of an internationalist. However, I liked these women for the most part. They had energy and were promoting important issues, particularly those concerning reproductive rights and social and economic equality.

Our visitor had a naturally intelligent curiosity and an independent spirit. At the time of her arrival, Iran was enmeshed in a war with the Kurds, some of whom were politically aligned with the Iraqis and some of whom were not.

The Kurds were a fascinating nation of people. Proud and resourceful, they had suffered greatly from attempts by the Shah and now the central government to exterminate their rich culture and history. During that time in mid-1980, our visitors loved Kurdistan because the Kurds were militant and exciting and actually engaged in a war with the central government's forces. They had firsthand accounts of the fighting. They had a strong warrior culture that our foreign guests found fascinating.

The Kurdish women wore brightly colored clothing, unlike the drab hijab of the city women. They fought alongside their men in battle. They contributed both heroic acts and martyrdom to a cause that had been going back for decades.

The political tourists loved meeting Kurdish fighters and would be welcomed to their villages where they were entertained by tribesmen sitting around shooting things and drinking vodka.

Not to be outdone, our feminist friend decided that she too would venture to Kurdistan. Decked out in her hijab, she boarded the bus to visit the Kurds. When she failed to return from her trip, I suspected the worst. Rumors travel quickly in Tehran. Someone told me she was in a provincial jail somewhere in the north but was being transported that day to the Central Prison in Tehran. Using my contacts at the Ministry of National Guidance, I was able to confirm that she was indeed sitting in a jail cell in Central Prison, hoping we all had noticed she was missing.

The funny thing about being raised in a country whose laws are based on the US Constitution is that you tend to make assumptions that others will adhere to roughly the same principles as you. For my part, I assumed my friend would be brought to Tehran and be released on her own recognizance, as she would be in America. I actually thought, I am chagrined to report, that after she had posted bail, she would simply be let out of jail pending a hearing. I expressed this to Hadj who was shocked by my naivety.

"So you think you are in America?" he asked. "You think that you can go and bail her out? No, no, Lisa*Khanuum*. That will not happen."

Hadj, not wanting to call unnecessary attention to himself, had to distance himself from this disaster. He could not intercede on this woman's behalf. He could not do anything to link himself to her trip. Our tourist pal had placed Hadj and his associates in a position of great risk. Her cavalier desire to have an "adventure" had real and deadly consequences for others; consequences she failed to adequately appreciate, I feared.

"*Khanuum*," Hadj began, "we need to come up with a plan that makes everyone think this is just one big mistake."

"But, I can't be involved at all and you need to make sure she sticks to the story. We have no idea what she has done or said while in jail. Act ignorant. Get to the point without getting to the point too quickly" he instructed.

I got it. I would arrange a visit with an official, and after the mandatory exchange of pleasantries, I would ask for help. The entire event was an innocent mistake, but the international ramifications might be greater. An American tourist held in an Iranian prison? That would certainly get the media's attention, I would insinuate. We wouldn't want that.

Our primary story would be simple: She was a friend from the United States, a tourist, who just wanted to see the countryside and got her wires crossed. She ended up hanging out in Kurdistan, not realizing anything controversial was going on there. I, her American friend, would pretend to be shamed and appalled by her silliness. I would set her straight. It was all one big mistake. She needed to leave. Let's not let this unfortunate incident turn into something more significant, I would implore.

My first stop was Sadegh, my friend, the Minister of National Guidance.

"*Agha* Sadegh," I started in slowly, after the first half hour of customary small talk about his family, my family, his work, my work and the weather. "We have a small problem. I need your help."

I described to him the circumstances surrounding my friend's arrest. "Clearly she had no idea where she was going. She simply wanted to see the sights in the north. There is so much more to Iran than Tehran, wouldn't you agree?"

Then I played the international incident card. I am relatively sure that the United States would have been unable to do anything to help this woman. It had already imposed a trade embargo and, more recently, a ban on travel to Iran by American citizens. However, I figured I had to appeal to Sadegh's more dramatic sensibilities and general ignorance of current US policies to get some help. I sat facing him, leaning ever so slightly forward, as if to tell him a secret.

"You know the media would love to use this incident to their advantage. They will use it as an excuse to further attack the revolution. The world will condemn Iran for holding this simple tourist woman. We must deal with this quietly before the news gets out. There are many reporters waiting outside. I have told no one about this. How can you help me?"

Sadegh, appearing pensive, looked briefly at the door, as if to see if anyone would be bursting in, lights flashing, scandal exposed.

"I think you need to speak with the Office of the President," he said, thoughtfully. "I think that is where the answer is."

The next day, armed with a box of cookies, I took a taxi to the Office of the President, the Honorable Abolhassan Bani Sadr.

I have told this story to many people who look at me like I am crazy. I tell them how I simply walked into the office of a man who was, for all intents and purposes, the vice president of the country, the president's right-hand man, and announced I was there to see the president. Clearly, Americans do not have the same easy access to their president. Nevertheless, that is exactly what I did. With all of the conviction I could muster, I walked into the building with my box of cookies and that can-do attitude my parents instilled in me as a child, pushing forward.

My friend had been arrested by provincial supporters of the more conservative Islamic fundamentalists. She faced the risk of being subjected to kangaroo court "trial" and then imprisoned. More than likely she would have been used as political capital in the constant battle between fundamentalism and the centrist agenda Bani Sadr's cronies espoused. Despite the deep divide between the US and Iran caused by the hostage crisis, elements within the Iranian government secretly sought an eventual and gradual normalization of relations, on Iran's terms of course. Any and every incident involving American citizens posed a distraction.

The Office of the President was located in a very official stone government building. The furniture was of the overly ornate baroque style favored by many wealthy Iranians. One entered through large wooden double doors to a waiting area with seats and coffee tables placed against the far wall. It was spacious and light. Three desks were positioned in a semicircle and behind each was an attractive woman, wearing the appropriate modest dress. I placed my cookies on the corner of the closest desk and announced that I would like to see Mr. Bani Sadr. All three women stood, staring at me. Graciously, I was asked to take a seat, and the women left the office through an adjoining door.

Apparently, the president was unavailable or a little too busy to meet personally with an unknown American visitor. I was relieved when his official representative, however, entered the room looking somewhat confused and perplexed at my presence in his offices. He greeted me by placing his right hand over his heart, while bowing his head slightly. This greeting replaced the more Western and often prohibited handshake with a woman. He motioned for me to sit facing him in an armchair. I complied. He placed himself on the small, ornate sofa in front of me, and leaned forward, thoughtfully, trying to comprehend why this woman had come to see the president.

"I want to thank you for taking the time to meet with me," I started. "I know you are busy. We have a problem that could become something very serious…internationally. I apologize for coming to the point so quickly…but this is serious."

"What is it?" he asked, slowly.

"My American friend, a woman, has been arrested by the Revolutionary Guards. She had gone to Kurdistan, perhaps ill-advisedly, and was arrested by provincial Revolutionary Guards. They have held her in a jail in the north somewhere. She was transferred yesterday to the Central Prison here. We need to get her out. I am afraid if the foreign press finds out about this, it will hurt what you are trying to do."

Hearing me out, he quickly understood the significance of my fears.

"Wait here," he said. "Wait. I will return."

It seemed to me he was gone for an eternity. As I waited impatiently, I watched the female assistants as they answered the phones and shuffled papers around their desks. Periodically I would catch one of them eyeing me with no small amount of curiosity. I would nod and smile.

He finally returned, holding paper and pen.

"I have confirmed that she has been transported to the Central Prison in Tehran," he declared sharply. "We will authorize her release. You must get her out of there."

He took up the paper and began to write. He signed it at the bottom with broad, circular strokes then, rising from his seat, he walked briskly to the desk of one of the female assistants. Handing her the sheet of paper, and with great dramatic flourish, she affixed a large stamped seal of the Office of the President at the bottom.

"Go and get her. Take her to the Hilton. You will be safe there," he ordered.

While I was initially perplexed by his instruction to take her to a specific hotel, he then informed me that former attorney general of the United States, Ramsey Clark, and a delegation of American intellectuals, parenthetically in violation of the US travel ban to Iran, were attending the Crimes of America conference of nonaligned countries at the Hilton Hotel organized by Bani Sadr that very week in June 1980. By sending us there, I immediately understood then that this particular event was supported, and better yet protected, by the forces loyal to Bani Sadr: The army and his faction within the government. My friend would, indeed, be safe there.

For the Americans attending this conference, held after the failed rescue attempt the previous April, their presence in Iran placed the entire delegation in danger of monetary sanctions and criminal prosecution from the US government. These individuals showed great courage in defying the travel ban to Iran. I can only presume they fell prey to heavy criticism upon their return.

"You will be the official US delegate to the conference," he told me. "As a delegate, your friend will not be at risk. This piece of paper will get you into the Hilton. Show it to the guards. They will make sure that you will not be detained or harassed by the others." I knew when he said "others" he meant the Revolutionary Guards who had arrested her and transported her to Tehran for their own purposes.

Document in hand, I rushed back to Sadegh's ministry. Sadegh knew I was coming, and had waiting for me a translator who spoke perfect idiomatic English, as we needed someone able to quickly communicate our plan to my friend. This guy fit the bill perfectly. He sounded like he had grown up in California.

Running out of Sadegh's building, the translator and I got into a taxi and headed downtown toward the Central Prison. It was hot, and the traffic was as horrific as usual. We chatted about banalities. I could tell he was nervous. I wore my bravado like a badge, and I tried to keep things light, despite the clear danger to him that he would enter the prison and not be allowed to leave.

He ordered the taxi to pull over and we exited on the sidewalk. The dull and imposing Central Prison could be seen directly across the busy roundabout teaming with cars and activity. Once we got out of the taxi, he had me wait on the sidewalk, while he went into a nearby antiques store.

When he came out he told me sternly, "Go into the shop. I told them you were with me on a tour—that I had to run an errand. They said they'd watch out for you while I was gone."

Looking terrified, he continued, "I am going into the prison. If I am not out with your friend in half an hour, that means they have arrested me. If that happens, I want you to get out of here as fast as you can. Get to the ministry and tell them to send someone to help me."

He was shaking. I went into the store, and did the "American tourist" browse—picking up old samovars and miniatures, admiring them, glancing out the window, and looking at my watch. It seemed to take forever for the hands on my watch to move.

All at once I saw the translator running from the building with my friend trailing behind him, wearing jeans and a scarf—running toward me, running for their lives. I flew out of the shop and met them on the sidewalk.

"Let's get the hell out of here," he yelled to us, over the din of the traffic. He hailed a cab and we sped off back to Sadegh's office.

My friend had been in jail for weeks—with no shower and little food. She smelled appalling and looked like she weighed ninety pounds—skin and bone. Dirty skin and bone, to be precise. I had assumed she'd need to change, and I'd brought clothes. Thankfully, one of the really great benefits of Islam is that toilets in Iran generally have water hoses in the stalls so that the devoted can wash themselves thoroughly before prayers.

Once we returned to the ministry, we retreated to the nearest ladies' room, and I hosed her down as best I could and shampooed her grimy hair. A change of clothes—four sizes too big but appropriate at least—and we were off to the Hilton.

The translator had bravely informed the authorities at the Central Prison that their prisoner was, in fact, the official representative of the United States of America who had been wrongly detained while traveling through "our glorious country" and that the President himself had issued an order that she be released. While he and my friend had been allowed to leave, we knew that we would be followed. Our pursuers made no attempt to hide themselves; two guys shoved into an Iranian-made sedan, watching and pointing at us as we exited the ministry building. I hailed a cab.

Almost jokingly I said, "Hey, we're going to the Hilton. We're being followed. Can you lose them?"

To my surprise, the face in the rearview mirror smiled and said, "You bet I can."

The drive from the ministry offices through the streets of Tehran was terrifying. The cab driver, apparently up for the adventure, drove full throttle in, around, behind and between cars. He sped the wrong way on small streets, and pressed his abundant luck by driving into oncoming cars. Zigzagging back and forth from west to east and then north, hunched over the steering wheel of his orange cab, he proved his potential as a stunt driver with us three pressed against the back of the rear seat, silently praying for the ride to stop. The hotel finally in sight, he proceeded to drive maniacally up the long, sweeping drive in front of the Tehran Hilton Hotel.

Uniformed soldiers at the checkpoint waved their rifles in the air and forced the car to a stop. Our shadows pulled over at the bottom of the drive, waiting and watching.

With the requisite amount of self-importance and flourish I handed the document prepared by the president's office to the guard. He motioned for us to stay in the car. Within minutes, an officer of some rank approached us. Opening the door, he asked us to get out and follow him into the hotel lobby. After some debate and discussion, it was decided that for her own safety my friend must stay at the hotel.

"We have a room for you," he announced. I did not tell him I had no intention of staying in the hotel; that my home was mere minutes away. My friend, however, was grateful to be given a shower and a bed, and the chance to organize her eventual departure from the country.

And so our participate as delegates began. We tried to attend the conference, really we did. But my friend hadn't eaten much in weeks, and I was suffering the effects of limited imported foods—very little sugar and almost no caffeine. And they certainly had food there. Lots and lots of food—free, sugary, sweet, fattening Western food. Cakes and cookies and vegetables I hadn't seen in months. And then, of course, they had coffee! We were in heaven. Clearly, someone put out the word to import a lot of food for the event, so the delegates would not learn the awful truth: Meat was priced like gold and vegetables were in extremely limited supply.

And so we sat and ate.

We mingled with the folks from various developing nations and national liberation movements. It was like being in some sort of radical heaven—with food. Clearly, no one had bothered to tell Ramsey Clark that he had two new delegates, nor were the other American delegates particularly welcoming when they found us tagging along on their official sightseeing junkets. The other Americans shunned us for the most part, but who could blame them? We just seemed to appear out of nowhere, did not participate in the actual conference, and spent most of our time hanging around the restaurant and coffee shop.

We did manage to accompany them on a tour of one of my favorite places in Iran. After a terrifying airplane ride from Tehran south to Esfahān (turbulence gone wild over the desert), our group deplaned slightly the worse for wear and was promptly shuttled onto waiting buses ready to take us into the city for a day of sightseeing. They were regular city buses, with few seats and bars to grasp as it lurched forward into the searing heat.

As our bus pulled onto the boulevard leading from the airport to the center of town, we were greeted by what appeared to be tens of thousands of well-wishers positioned on each side of the road, waving signs and yelling slogans. The delegates recoiled in horror at the sight of the chanting citizens, and I suspect they feared the buses would be attacked. Assuming that the delegates understood this was meant to be a welcoming gesture, the handlers traveling with us said nothing to the group to dispel this fear.

"They are chanting 'Welcome, Friends,'" I mentioned casually to the terrified American woman standing nearest to me. "Don't be afraid," I said, attempting to comfort her. She just looked at me and said nothing.

Just as I had fallen prey to my deeply imbedded assumptions about the Iranian judicial system, these delegates appeared to have been influenced by shots of thousands of chanting protesters burning American flags and violently scaling the walls of the US embassy. It was hard for any American at the time to understand that the Iranian people did not hate the US.

Even after the 1953 coup that replaced their beloved, popularly elected leader with the repressive Shah; even after the students seizing the US embassy had discovered, by piecing together official documents, irrefutable evidence in the US embassy that the United States had again been meddling in a plot to overthrow Khomeini. Despite all this, the average Iranian did not hate Americans.

It was not uncommon for me to be accosted by little old ladies on the street who would grab at me, pulling my face down toward theirs to kiss my cheeks.

"Tell Jimmy Carter," they would exclaim, breathlessly. "Tell Jimmy Carter and your mother, you are safe here. Tell them we love your people."

It was endearing but I never really had the heart to tell them that I didn't have the same access to Jimmy Carter that I apparently had to the president of Iran. Sadly, I couldn't just walk into Jimmy's office and give him the message.

At the conclusion of the Crimes of America conference, my friend was escorted to the airport and placed on a plane bound for California. She had stayed the entire conference in the relative security of the hotel, surrounded by a military loyal to centrist president Bani Sadr.

I visited with her daily, always making sure to do what I imagined a secret agent would do to lose "a tail" when I left the hotel: catching a taxi at the hotel, I would travel in the opposite direction of my home, cut through a narrow alley, walk through a shop to the back, double back, and then finally take a bus up the boulevard to my street.

I had hoped that my presence with the mystery American delegate would go unnoticed. It had not.

CHAPTER 19
HUNTER, GATHERER, MEDICINE WOMAN

By the Fall of 1980, the war between Iran and Iraq had created the illusion of national unity. At that time, Saddam Hussein and Iraq were staunch allies of the United States and were using newly minted US made weapons to attack Iran. The new Iranian regime loudly proclaimed it to be a proxy war created by the US and calculated to weaken the Islamic Republic. Decades of conflict over land, religion and regional power came to a head. And, after commencing initially with some skirmishes earlier in the year, fighting began in earnest on September 22, 1980 with Iraqi forces invading southern Iran. Iran had been invaded and the people rallied to its defense ready to sacrifice themselves as martyrs to Shi'a Islam.

During that time, air-raid sirens would go off at night, reminiscent of the London Blitz. And searchlights would cut through the dark, seeking out offending enemy aircraft. Periodically, the sirens would sound in the middle of the day and people scrambled into the nearest arched doorway or open, available basement. More than once, I found myself pressed up against the stone facade of a downtown building, waiting for the siren to stop or the sound of an explosion to assault my ears. Thankfully, no bombs landed in downtown Tehran, but the fear brought on by the siren's wail was paralyzing.

I like to tell people that Hadj alone was personally responsible for starting the trend of taping windows in our neighborhood, as he stood on the sidewalk one day placing large Xs across each pane of glass.

"If a bomb drops near us, it creates a vacuum and they will implode," he announced with great authority. "This will stop the glass from falling on us." Within weeks everyone on our street had large Xs covering their windows as well.

From the balcony of Iranzamin School in the western part of the city, where I continued to work as a teacher, we could see Iraqi jets in dogfights with US-supplied, Shah-era Iranian F-14s in the skies to the west. They would chase each other like birds across the sky.

A couple of times the Iraqis successfully bombed factories on the outskirts of eastern Tehran. Periodic incursions into Tehran's airspace would be met with thunderous rebuttals by Iranian 20-millimeter anti-aircraft guns perched on the ridge above our house. We would stand on the roof of our home on those nights, watching the perverted fireworks display of the anti-aircraft guns, waiting and watching to see if our house would get bombed.

Common sense dictates that you should shelter in the basement during a bombing attack. In our house, however, the basement was where we kept the oil, gas and propane. I had decided early on I preferred a quick death to a slow burn, so we took to the rooftop.

In an effort to build national unity, after each threat of attack by Iraqi planes or on the anniversary of some significant political event, the citizens were encouraged to run to the rooftop and yell, *"Allah O Akbar! Khomeini Ra'h Bar"* (God is Great! Khomeini is our Leader!). This chanting would always take place after the evening call to prayers as the sun set each night. To amuse ourselves, Hadj and I (along with many others) would yell out at the top of our lungs, *"Allah O Akbar! Khomeini Ah Magk."* This, roughly translated, means "God is great. Khomeini is an asshole!" This silly little act of defiance amused us greatly.

"Will anyone tell on us?" I asked Hadj, smiling.

"No, Lisa*Khanuum*," he replied, amused. "And, if they do, I will just tell them it's just how Americans pronounce *Ra'h Bar*."

"Umm, good plan. Blame the accent."

Aside from the blackouts, the war brought with it more intense rationing. Meat, gasoline, heating fuel, and medication were all in short supply. Butter and milk were reserved for the poor, who mostly lived in south Tehran.

There was also an intense atmosphere of suspicion and fear; fear of collaborators and fear of anti-Islamic Republic sentiment. Our garbage collector routinely reported the comings and goings at our house—by virtue of any sudden increase in our trash. The mailman had to be routinely bribed to bring me my mail.

There were other indignities as well. On a weekly basis our water would be turned off. The tap would begin to trickle, and I would rush out and fill buckets from the fountain. Then as quickly as it went off, it would suddenly and inexplicably return. For no apparent reason, the electricity would shut off; always, as I said, in the northern parts of the city. There was no rhyme or reason to this except, of course, the northern neighborhoods were where the wealthy lived. The government authorities just wanted to mess with the rich folks and turning off our power or water was just the ticket.

One day, Hadj came home, almost vibrating with excitement. One of his friends had a contract with the government to construct some buildings. This meant he needed to hire a lot of workers and those workers needed to be fed. This meant chicken! The government allowed him to import a container of whole, unbutchered fresh chickens.

His friend had called and offered up a dozen chickens for our eating enjoyment. The catch was, of course, that we had to run the roadblock gauntlet in the middle of the night, pick them up, and get them home—without being stopped by the Revolutionary Guard. It was a daunting task, but we were up for the challenge.

We placed two huge plastic tubs in the trunk of the precious 1972 white Mercedes Hadj's father had left us to protect with our lives. We filled the tubs with ice and headed out at 2 a.m. We were lucky to encounter no roadblocks. We recklessly drove the wrong way down one-way streets, hoping no one else would be on the road at that hour.

I was elated when we arrived, unnoticed, at his friend's high-rise apartment. Entering the apartment, the smell of raw chicken was overwhelming. There were hundreds of dead chickens, filling scores of huge plastic tubs of ice, not unlike ours.

"They let me bring in a container for my men," he declared with pride. "I have called everyone I know. Take some. Have some."

We loaded up.

After Hadj and his friend had carefully and quietly taken our tubs back down the stairs, gently placing them in the trunk of the car, we headed off home. The ride home was far more stressful than the ride there, because we were transporting contraband chicken. Avoiding all of the main roads and again driving the wrong way down one-way streets, we eventually made our way home. I jumped out of the car, opened the metal door to the carport, and Hadj eased the car into its spot.

Over the next six hours, I learned more than I ever wanted to learn about gutting a chicken. As Hadj had to put in one of his twelve-hour shifts the following day, I volunteered to stay up, clean, cut, pack, and freeze our prize.

First, the chickens had to be washed. Then the orphaned feathers had to be plucked out. Thankfully, these chickens were headless—not like the ones I bought at the chicken store, where customers would walk in, designate a victim, and watch as the subject was removed to the back of the shop, executed without due process, run through some mysterious plucking device, and then placed warm in a plastic bag. Those chickens gave me the creeps.

Although headless, our new chickens were, alas, untouched. I needed to gut them and gut them fast. I became the Wizard of the Gizzard. I isolated and removed the green bile sack like a pro. This was particularly true after my fourth hour of gutting and cutting. I had no previous experience cutting up dead things. Again, my mother-in-law—the fount of all food knowledge—had carefully shown me what parts to use and what to avoid. She was very clear: cut the bile sack, ruin the meat. God forbid I should ruin this meat. We had risked our lives for these damned birds. I became a surgeon, gutting and cutting with robotic precision.

It was a real shame my in-laws were out of town. My mother-in-law would have been tickled at my chicken-butchering prowess. My father-in-law would have been up all night, pacing and worrying, fearing either eminent death by firing squad for receiving bootleg chickens or, worse, chicken juice in the trunk of the beloved Mercedes.

Once packed and sacked, I froze our chicken in handy, meal-size portions. This, I figured, was my particular homage to the American way of doing things. In Iran, one simply cooks the entire bird. After all, a guest might appear at your home at dinnertime; someone might drop in, and he or she must be fed. I figured in that case I'd defrost another bag.

I felt particularly satisfied with myself as I fell into bed that night, ready to seize the day and create new and exciting hybrid Amero-Iranian foods with my cache of bootleg chicken. Another adventure to add to my growing list.

It was hugely inconvenient and generally annoying, but I was actually somewhat sympathetic. The knee-jerk liberal part of my brain allowed me to rationalize why the *haves* should experience having to be the *have nots* from time to time.

As usual in Iran, when faced with a challenge or confronted with a limitation, someone will find a way around it. This was the rebel way that I so enthusiastically embraced. When meat was rationed, I bought it on the black market from guys selling dead chickens in trashcans full of ice. They would suddenly appear on the street, and the word would spread like wildfire.

"Hurry up! I saw a chicken guy in front of the *ma'hroseh* (store). Hurry up, let's go get some," said my friend, breathlessly ringing my doorbell.

Donning our head scarves, we'd run with our plastic bags in hand down the hill to the local corner store, where a guy with a fifty-gallon trash can filled with ice stood bargaining away freshly slaughtered chickens. We outbid all takers, frantically waving our money in his face.

Returning home, I guarded my prize proudly. The fact that I had paid the equivalent of twenty bucks for this scrawny, two-pound bird was irrelevant. I had scored a chicken. I would cut it up and scatter it over our rice and beans. It would last us a week. It was a good day. I was a good hunter.

Getting eggs could also be quite an adventure. Often while driving up the freeway toward our home, we would see a truck swerve off to the side of the road and stop abruptly. The driver would dash out to the back, throw up the tailgate, and expose his precious cargo of flats and flats of fresh eggs.

Invariably, a traffic jam would result as frantic shoppers screeched to a halt, in the hopes of buying a flat of eggs. Hadj and I were savvy shoppers and we'd often manage to score some eggs. I'd hold them on my lap like a new puppy as we drove home through the mass of traffic.

During one of these freeway shopping trips, I noticed a crowd had formed around something or someone lying on the ground. As Hadj and I approached, I noticed a man who was clearly in the throes of a grand mal seizure writhing on the hot asphalt.

"Get him up!" I commanded, spontaneously. "Get him off the ground!"

The crowd turned in unison and stared with open confusion and a certain amount of contempt at the American woman telling them what to do.

"Get him up off the ground," I repeated. "The asphalt is burning his skin!" They just looked at me.

"She is a doctor," Hadj lied. "Do what she says."

Amazingly, they did just that. Amid yelling, screaming, pushing, and shoving, men in gray sport coats and rubber slippers were directing and assisting. Within a few minutes, the crowd had managed to pick up the man and shove him into a waiting car. Off to the hospital he went.

"They think he's possessed," said Hadj, matter-of-factly.

"No, they don't," I said, incredulously. "They know it's a seizure."

"Well, some know, but some think it's the devil." Then he laughed, "The 'devil' American doctor told them what do to."

He laughed and laughed as we drove home.

I learned to use the phrase again with a man who had a seizure right in front of my house. Our doorbell rang, and I opened the door to find a man panicked and pointing furiously at his friend on the ground.

"Turn him on his side," I ordered. "Do not put anything in his mouth. He is almost done. I am a doctor," I lied, emphatically.

I got this information from watching television and from taking a couple of first aid classes in the United States. Happily, the man recovered from his seizure, and I told his friend to take him to see a real doctor, only I didn't say real doctor. I said "his doctor." They drove off. Dr. Lisa, American Medicine Woman, had saved the day.

When you are living in scarcity, you learn either make do or do without. You adapt. You make some sacrifices. You get over yourself and prioritize your needs. It was during this war period that Hadj came down with a horrible case of gastroenteritis. He was as sick as they come. Apparently, he had decided to throw caution to the wind and, along with the folks downtown, eat stuff he bought off the streets.

Like any large city, the streets of Tehran are filled with vendors hawking foods and drinks. In the winter they would sell hot chestnuts and delicious grilled corn on the cob. In the summer, fruity drinks or yogurt sodas were always available. A customer would stop at the vendor's cart, drink from a communal glass, and return it to the vendor. After a cursory rinse off, it was refilled and ready for the next customer. It was a germ-filled proposition, but I figured it was also a good way to build my immunity against stomach upset. I never got really sick. I did get vaguely, slightly, sort of queasy once in a while. It was my diet plan—the food, the germs, and the exercise caused the pounds to drop off me like water down a rosebush. I had never been healthier. The same could not be said for Hadj. He ate lunch one day in a local workingman's eatery. The food—cheap and hearty—consisted of a meat stew cooked for days, mixed with turmeric and other spices, chickpeas, and served with rice. It was delicious stuff.

The restaurant was always crowded, and the tables sticky. Lord knows how the plates were washed. Who looked? But Hadj ate there and almost died. He could hold nothing down. He became severely dehydrated, weak, and nonresponsive.

I had taken a private class before leaving for Iran from a woman who had been a field nurse in Vietnam on the off chance I would be called upon to conduct a field amputation or deliver a baby or sew up a wound. Luckily, I never had to sever a limb or bring new life into the world, but that lesson on inserting an IV came in handy that day.

In Iran, the local drugstore is the source of pretty much any drug or medical apparatus, so in desperation I ran down the hill to the drugstore next to the general store and flew through the door.

"I need IV glucose and an IV setup," I demanded, unceremoniously.

"Of course," responded the pharmacist. "You must be the American doctor."

Word apparently travels fast, I thought. I didn't deny it. Had I needed syringes, heroin, morphine, or quaaludes, I am pretty sure he would have given them to me too.

I ran back up the hill to the house and found Hadj being examined by a real doctor, a family friend.

"Well," he opined. "He is sick."

"Thanks," I replied.

I presented the doctor with the IV setup, something to hydrate him, and he recoiled. He had not, it appeared, actually inserted an IV in decades. Perhaps since medical school. I grabbed Hadj's hand, felt for the largest vein on the back of it, and slowly inserted the needle, feeling for the flash.

When the tubing attached to the needle began to color with Hadj's blood, I inserted the unit into the IV bag, hung it from a lamp, taped down the needle, and waited. The doctor was clearly impressed. And to be honest, I was pretty impressed with myself as well.

After a few days Hadj finally recovered, a little worse for wear. His bout with food poisoning, however, did not stop him from frequenting small local restaurants and coffee shops. He figured that together we would just find a way to deal with it.

CHAPTER 20
WARDROBE MALFUNCTIONS

It was against this backdrop of political turmoil, I discovered, to my delight, that I was pregnant in the spring of 1981. I remember that day, Hadj and I were out and about, getting an official document stamped or approved and walking down the long, narrow alleys that pass for streets in Tehran. These *ku chehs* sprouted like veins from the main thoroughfare running north to south. I had been overcome by some mysterious illness and ended up losing my breakfast in a ditch directly outside the ministry. A few weeks later, it was official. My mysterious illness was morning sickness.

In 1981, women were opting for natural childbirth in the United States, but Iranian women wanted all the drugs they could handle. I found myself a Johns Hopkins–trained OB-Gyn and announced defiantly to him that I would be having a natural birth. I assumed that there would be Lamaze classes all over town. I assumed wrong. I was on my own. I found a used paperback book on natural childbirth written by a British midwife. Her message was simple: do what you would normally do to relieve the stress of childbirth, breathe, and relax. For me, it happened to be singing.

Pregnant and on the hunt for maternity wear in my size, I ventured down our hill to the market in search of large lady panties to encase my growing baby belly. I had discovered I had a talent for using our peddle sewing machine to create billowing jumpers and smocked tunics that served as appropriate pregnancy garments. But while the *roo pusht* (cover up) may be the perfect maternity wear, a lady still needs to wear undies.

I had seen a women's clothing stall in the market and approached it, with some trepidation. I did not know the actual word for underwear as it had never come up in a conversation with anyone at any time and for any reason. I was relieved to see no word was needed. There they were, nicely laid out before me, a veritable cornucopia of granny panties. I was amused to see the brand name was "US Pretty Lady," written in English to perhaps suggest they were imported. How charming. We were meant to find each other.

I picked out four pairs and felt rather proud of my negotiating skills when I was able to get them for what I thought was a fair price. Excited and armed with my new purchase, I rushed back up the hill to try them on.

My granny panties became a metaphor for the contradiction between the Iranian desire for self-realization and self-reliance as a nation and the insidious need that to imitate all things Western that had, ironically, become a forceful impetus of the revolution. US Pretty Lady panties—the name said it all. I wore them with pride. I had no others that would fit. I wore them right up to the day they fell off unceremoniously as I waddled down Mossadegh Avenue.

As is often the case with imitators, the overall quality of the garment was lacking. The thought was good, but alas, the execution was very poor. And thus, as I was walking down Mossadegh Avenue on my way home after a wholly uneventful visit to the only supermarket in town, the elastic on my US Pretty Lady panties gave way and they fell to my ankles. Fearing the worst and without missing a beat, I simply stepped out of them, and experienced that ultimate freedom of going commando. I was liberated! My panties lay dead and lifeless on the sidewalk, the tragic victim of poor-quality construction.

For me, pregnancy was the mother of invention. I could not find a single pair of maternity pants in my size in Tehran. I had, as I said, been able to fashion a few maternity smocks but no pants. In a moment of brilliant ingenuity, I found that by stringing a large rubber band between the button and buttonhole of my jeans, I was able to expand the waistbands of my pants to cover my growing girth.

When one enters a shop in Iran, if there are others waiting to be served, the customer must aggressively wave money back and forth in front of the shopkeeper to get his attention. Once served, the customer must then once more wave the bills until they are taken. Change is given and, once pocketed, the transaction is complete.

I found this entire money waving process intimidating and odd. The lack of attention to customer service was off-putting initially. But like most things, I gradually got used to it.

I'd discovered a bakery about a mile from our home that made delicious apple turnovers and set out on an adventure to buy a dozen or so. I entered the store, clutching my purse in one hand and expertly waving my money in the other.

"*Beyfarmayeen! Khanuum!*" I shouted above the crowd.

Getting the attention of the clearly apathetic woman behind the counter, I ordered my pastries. She turned and placed them into a box, closed it with string, and put it on the counter. Fearful that some other customer would snag my wares, I grabbed the box with the hand still holding the cash and again waved it at the saleslady.

After an excessive amount of time and waving, she finally dispossessed me of my money. And then it happened. Again. With one short twang, my rubber band broke and my jeans dropped to the ground around my ankles.

As my arms were now filled with my box of sweets and my purse, it took me an eternity to modestly pull my pants up over my rear end. Pressing the front of my pants to my pregnant belly, I proceeded to waddle out the door to the sidewalk for the trek home.

The other customers, to their credit, simply chose to ignore my distress even after I started to laugh maniacally at my predicament. I managed to make it back home, this time without leaving my garment on the sidewalk but with yet another amusing tale of my adventures to tell my long-suffering in-laws.

I had taken up knitting. With no television and a need to keep busy, I was drawn to all of the womanly arts. I knitted. I sewed. I designed my own versions of appropriate Muslim women's wear. I made tunics and smocks. I knitted a sweater. I had no pattern and minimal prior experience. My father—who had proudly learned the fine arts of knitting and crocheting from his mother—had taught me. My mother, little princess that she was, had never really taken to such things.

I enjoyed the adventure of the hunt and the joy of the project. I would set out early in the day in search of the wool shop or the fabric store. I would ask taxi drivers, family and friends. I would walk for miles down city streets, stopping only to peer up at signs. I would attempt to translate from the script into my developing Persian. It was a painful process, but I had the time.

I was overjoyed to discover a wool shop relatively close to the house and promptly purchased a number of skeins of white wool. I set about making myself a knit garment of some sort. Everyone was sure I was a little crazy but kept the negative comments to themselves. It didn't take me long to finish the prize. It was fabulous. I had not bothered to measure anything, so the sleeves came down at least eight inches from the tips of my fingers. I rolled them up. The sweater itself, appropriately, I believe, hung down to my knees. I was nearly eight months pregnant at the time. It was freezing outside in December 1981, and I had the ultimate knitted *roo pusht*. I was absolutely sure all the ladies would be jealous.

Imbued with a newly discovered confidence, I set off to make myself a jaunty matching cap. I was able to fabricate an actual knit cap, again in white wool. The two pieces together formed the basis of my winter *hijab*. I thought I looked rather fetching; the family was not convinced.

I regularly wore my outfit, donning my knit ensemble and hitting the streets. One day, standing on the bus as it inched down Mossadegh, I heard a man and a woman whispering about me behind my back. I turned and smiled. They responded by smiling broadly back at me. Then, still grinning, the man said to the woman in a stage whisper, "What is that? Is that a man or a woman?"

Now in his defense, you have to picture me on that day. I was dressed in jeans and my favorite clogs. I was wearing my kicky knit tunic and matching cap, pulled modestly down to my forehead. I was enormously pregnant and resembled, I have to admit, a giant walking snowball.

"I am a woman," I replied, somewhat sheepishly.

This experience didn't dampen my enthusiasm for the knit outfit, however. Despite the strange stares, and the obvious amusement, that uniquely American side of me—that side of me that needed, demanded, required I be an individual—continued to shine through.

CHAPTER 21
ORPHAN INFORMANT

One sunny afternoon in mid-1981, Hadj brought a boy home. His name was Omran. It was never made clear to me who he was. I thought he was an orphan. He had some relationship to someone who worked with someone related to someone—Hadj felt he needed some help.

"He's a good kid," Hadj said. "He can live here, help out. You'll see. It will be good." And with that, he planted the child with me and went off to work.

That is, of course, very Iranian. It is kind of a private welfare system. The poor are brought into a home to work. If they stay loyal for any significant period of time, a bond is created. The rich take care of the poor. Omran was, I would guess, about thirteen years old. He was short and just a little grimy. Like most working-class kids, he wore baggy dark pants, rubber slippers, and a baggy white shirt. His hair was kept short in a buzz cut. His eyes were bright and alive. He didn't seem to miss anything, even though he always pretended not to hear me. I wasn't really very keen on the idea of a servant of any sort. Having a stranger in my house, watching me, and under my control weirded me out.

By the end of fall Omran proved to be rather problematic. He was lazy, which I chose to ignore most of the time, as I was loathe to ask him to do anything. He seemed to spend a lot of time watching me move around the house doing stuff. He rarely spoke; he just watched.

Pregnant, I had taken a leave of absence from the international school. I didn't want to risk being exposed to some hideous, childhood illness unintentionally, of course, passed to me by one of my little boys. I had seen how—as crammed together as the children were in the classroom—one flu bug could wipe out an entire row. I didn't want to take that chance. So I stayed home, nesting, and filled my days by giving private English lessons. I filled my nights typing hand-written translations on my IBM Selectric, and all the time I suspected that Omran was spying on me.

I cannot remember the exact date, but I do recall that Omran and Hadj had had an argument that day. Hadj, who was just trying to help the kid out, was angry and frustrated at the arrogance and inso lence the child displayed. It was bad enough that he was completely unresponsive to me, but when he displayed the same attitude with Hadj, enough was enough.

Hadj was the kind of man who thought anyone could be made to understand—to see the truth of what he was saying. He would approach the resistant person, place his arm around his shoulder, and draw him into his sphere of power. Slowly, forcefully, he would repeat his position, his stance, his take, his opinion over and over again, until the victim subtly surrendered. Hadj liked to get his way.

His message was one of hope and cooperation and working together for a better future. He was always trying to appeal to the higher self in each person. Hadj wanted Omran to appreciate the best of himself—to live his best life, to help out the pregnant American woman. Hadj's philosophy was grounded in his political belief that common men, working together for the common good and following a common plan, would produce a better society.

I appreciated his approach, but his lofty ideals were lost on most folks. It's just too hard to think about others all the time. It's just too hard to be involved, to advocate.

Hadj's appeal to Omran apparently fell on deaf ears. The kid was an opportunist. When the discussion deteriorated into a shouting match, with Hadj saying something equivalent to, "you selfish little bastard!" Omran ran out the front door.

I had no idea where he went and, frankly, I didn't care. I was glad that he'd gone. Little did I know Omran seemed to live by the motto: "Don't get mad, get even." He ran directly to the local vigilantes. Armed with stories of strange comings and goings in our house, emboldened by the fact that an American lived there, he had decided that he would honor his patriotic duty to bite the hand that had been feeding him, and he turned us in. And so, in the middle of the night, they came for Hadj.

The knock on our front door echoed through our foyer, carried over the marble floors, and filled the house. We could see the outline of several bodies as we turned on the light that illuminated the outside of our home. We could see they were armed—the silhouettes of rifles clearly visible through the frosted glass.

Hadj opened the door slowly as I stood holding my scarf over my head, wrapped in my floor-length bathrobe. He looked back at me, and motioned me to stay in the bedroom. Do not come out, his eyes said. Do not speak. Do not move. Just stay where you are.

There's always a leader with these groups of men. He's the one who talks, commands, gives orders. The followers stand behind him, looking menacing. They have power, of course, because they have the guns. They know this. It makes them cocky. It makes them skittish. They must be handled, at all times, very carefully.

With the requisite amount of feigned deference, Hadj asked them what they were doing there at this time of night, in his home.

"*Agha*," said the designated leader. "Come with us. Now."

Hadj needed no other explanation. This was it. They were taking him in. They had found out about the factory, our school, the political work. Had it been our garbage man? Had he divined by inspecting our garbage that we had too many guests? Did my mailman turn on me? Was it that little shit, Omran?

The current state of repression and revenge being perpetrated against anyone who sought to oppose the regime had made neighbor turn on neighbor. I had no idea if I would ever see him again. I had no idea if I would be next. Should I leave now? Should I pack? Where could I go? Would I have my child in prison? My mind began to race. I had my US passport carefully hidden under the bathroom sink, duct-taped to the pipes. I wasn't taking any chances with that. Should I run to the Swiss? Could I run? If he didn't come back, I just couldn't leave, could I? What should I do? What would Hadj want me to do?

You would have thought he and I would have had a contingency plan in place the entire time we were in Iran. Wrong. I have no idea why we never discussed the possibility of his arrest or, worse yet, execution. But Hadj never thought we'd need a plan. Just as my youth made me feel somewhat invincible, Hadj's experience and passion made him believe he could work his way out of any situation. Mostly he could. He was, of course, a charmer.

During his decades spent building coalitions and support for his cause, he could, by virtue of his powerful charisma, will people to do what he wanted. He was particularly effective with the liberal church-lady types, who would literally swoon over him. For them, he was the closest thing to a romantic revolutionary they would ever meet. God help him, I hoped he'd be able to use his charms now.

The village above our neighborhood had its own militia—the *Basij*. This group, which was originally a neighborhood organization formed during the Iraq war, was supposedly formed to protect against an Iraqi invasion. Male and female volunteers would meet regularly and learn how to assemble and disassemble AK-47s. They would practice crawling under barbed wire, hiking up the mountain, doing paramilitary physical-training exercises.

However, the *Basij* eventually morphed into a group of paid professionals. Scary, empowered, well-financed, gun-toting idiots. They were ignorant people with little or no real-life experience beyond their little villages or neighborhoods. And I would bet good money that our school's morality monitor, who himself was a member of the *Basij*, had never even met foreigners before being assigned to spy on us at the international school.

Some *Basij* were paid professionals, but most were volunteers. The rank and file joined, I am sure, because they felt a patriotic pull to protect the motherland. This type of volunteerism is really admirable. It is good to want to protect your people, but the passage of time mutated that sentiment into the black uniformed brutes that they became—the murderous, thuggish gangs that roam the streets.

So while the men who took Hadj that night had yet to become professional enforcers, they were still capable of having him imprisoned or worse.

I sat up that night, not so much waiting as going over my options. I didn't know that Omran was responsible for the visit. I had no idea what had happened—who had told or why. Our no-need-to-know policy kept me out of the loop. I could only assume the worst and plan for it.

First, I went into the apartment and collected every photograph I could find—any photo of anyone we knew. My in-laws had left Iran for a period of time, and Hadj and I were staying in the main house. The apartment served as my classroom and office. I had my papers there and, of course, my typewriter.

In the dark of the blackout, I fumbled around for anything I thought could link us to anyone else. I collected our wedding photos, featuring the smiling faces of friends who could be implicated. Handwritten transcripts that had been translated into English from Farsi and given to me for typing were swept into bags. Letters from home—innocent, but foreign—were shredded. I collected everything I could find. I knew this time I could not burn and bury them. I could not risk calling attention to myself or the house with a plume of smoke in the middle of the night.

What to do? I agonized.

Flush. Page after page, photo after photo, I tore each and every one into tiny bits. I placed the bits into a pot of hot water, hoping this would help disintegrate them. I created a paste. Then flush by flush, hour by hour I released my memories into the vast sewer system.

The sheer length of time it took me to collect, reduce, and refuse the paper served to take my mind off my abject fear. It gave me something to do other than worry. It was mindless, and thus my mind was free to plan.

I would wait, I thought. Then I would send someone from the religious side of the family—someone beyond reproach, someone respected—to visit the captors. Family is family, and politics aside, they would do this. Even though some of them had hated vehemently everything Hadj had done in the United States—everything he stood for—he was still family. They protect the family name. And despite all of the apologist verbiage they would say to justify the excesses of the Islamic Republic, they would do it to avoid the stink of Hadj's capture from invading their homes. Selfless, perhaps. Self-interested, for sure. So I would approach them, and they would do this thing. I would not go with them, of course. We would not want to rub my nationality into the faces of the ill-informed.

Once I knew what Hadj's fate would be, then I would stay. I would stay and—or so I thought arrogantly—work in and among those of my contacts within the government who had not been shot during this latest political purge to get Hadjut. Perhaps, I thought, I would make this into an international scandal. How naïve I was, in retrospect. As if the foreign press would give a damn about yet another Iranian man killed for believing the wrong thing at the wrong time.

As the sun came up, I sat silently in the kitchen, drinking weak tea and wondering how I would raise our soon-to-be-born child alone. I was resigned to the realization that I would need to return to California if my worst fears were realized. Once I knew what was happening to Hadj—once *something* had happened—I would need to return to California. Could I stay here among murderers? It was doubtful.

I did not see him approach the house, but I heard the loud metal clang of the front door closing. Hadj was back! I ran to him, bursting into spontaneous sobs, breathless, clinging to his neck, my face buried on his shoulder.

"Oh my God!" I wailed. "What happened? Are you okay? Did they hurt you?" I peppered him with questions.

"That son of a bitch, Omran," he mumbled. "He turned me in. He went to those assholes, and told them something fishy was going on here."

"What did you say?" I asked.

"I told them nothing was going on. I said that I was just trying to help him out. I told them he was just making trouble. Rahim vouched for me."

Hadj's brother-in-law, Rahim, was a warm and quiet man, highly and very privately religious. He was a constant fixture at the local mosque. He was, as they say, above suspicion. He was not overtly political, and made few, if any, contributions to the political arguments that would periodically erupt during twilight teas and family parties. He was a gentle soul and enormously respected as a man of honor.

"How did he find out about this?" I asked, confused.

"I told them he would vouch for me. They got him this morning. He came, he vouched, and they let me go."

"Shit! I was sweating bullets," I exclaimed. "I cut up and flushed all my work—all of our pictures!"

"Good," said Hadj. "We need a plan, Lisa*Khanuum*. We need a plan now."

Plan A: No more quasi "we think they are needy" orphans at our house.

Plan B: Be more careful.

CHAPTER 22
TOO MUCH, TOO SOON

Nothing can really prepare you for the sound of gunfire, the smell of burning tires, the smell of warm blood. Nothing. Walking the streets of Tehran in those days, I had experienced them all. It was not uncommon to turn the corner of a small street and find bodies laid out in a neat row, in plain view, loosely covered with sheets; now deceased members of one opposition group or another on display as a cautionary tale for others to see.

The revolution that culminated in February 1979 was soon followed by the embassy seizure nine months later. The tide of politics shifted almost daily. The tension heightened with the Iran-Iraq war. New traitors were declared, ministries were purged, men and women were shot.

Between 1979 and 1981, the streets were routinely filled with demonstrators. Groups of men and women took to the streets, all hoping to influence those in power. Sometimes groups would dare to resist, taking up arms and engaging in skirmishes with Revolutionary Guards. They were roundly crushed.

Most of the armed uprisings were ill-conceived and ill-timed. They resulted in many deaths, but little of consequence. There were bombs and bombings, abandoned briefcases—bags would explode in the doorways of consulates, businesses, and ministries. Caution was the name of the game. The war with Iraq, started in September 1980 and in full swing by 1981, and the political tide was turning in favor of the fundamentalists. Nothing creates patriotic idiocy more than a good war.

I would walk home in the early evenings, positioning myself on the boulevard in order to hail a taxi, and the air would fill with the sound of sirens. The Iraqi fighter jets would fly overhead. They would appear to cut their engines, creating a startling and unexpected moment of silence. It was that silence that terrified me as I had been told that cutting the engines was a precursor to dropping their payloads. I would step into a doorway and wait for the blast that did not come. It was a terrifying game.

It was now 1981. For months, the political rivalries and purges that characterized the tug-of-war between various factions in the government raged on. The more "moderate" supporters of Bani Sadr engaged in fierce ideological battles with forces supporting hard-right fundamentalism. In the US, this type of jockeying for power is often manifested by attack ads appearing on television or questionable news stories planted strategically in newspapers or television specifically aimed at discrediting one political figure or another. In Iran, the consequences of dissent or falling out of favor were and remain far more lethal.

An allegation of disloyalty to "the revolution," that vague and broad catch-all charge, could lead to long-term imprisonment or death by unceremonious execution. Even those who supported Khomeini originally were not immune from political purges and imprisonment.

For those who supported the movement for democracy in Iran, this period of upheaval and discord among the ruling clerics was seen as an opportunity to step in in the hopes that a viable alternative would emerge from the rubble.

"Remember, Lisa*khanuum*," Hadj would declare, "you have to break eggs to make an omelet."

"But," he continued, "we can't just swoop in like we are saviors and tell people what to do. The people need to be ready to fight and die. They are not there yet."

I had created this ridiculous fantasy in my head that Hadj and I would, when the time was right and passions were sufficiently aroused, inspire all of our wealthy neighbors to risk everything and "liberate" our neighborhood. We would march as one, unified force, and seize the television station located a few short blocks from our homes. It was a glorious fantasy. We would control the media and issue a call to arms. Inspirational military music would be played in the background as the announcer extolled the citizens to rise up!

"We need to be ready," I announced to Hadj, after sharing my *Les Miserables* plan with him.

The evening air was cooling from the day's heat and we positioned ourselves in comfortable chairs on our marble terrace, overlooking the expanse of our walled garden. As the fountain serenaded us with the sound of gently falling water, we sipped our tea and tried to make plans.

"I have no idea what to do," I complained. "No one tells me anything."

"You don't need to know anything. You shouldn't know anything," he replied.

"But I have been collecting soda bottles!" I protested. "Behrooz came over and told us how to make Molotov cocktails with them."

"Lisa*khanuum,*" he said, head lowered with an ill-hidden bemused smile, "really? Do you really think you are ready to lead a charge? You?" He laughed softly, reaching out and gently placing his hand on my arm to reassure me that while he thought my idea was insane, he knew my heart was in the right place.

"It is too soon," Hadj declared. "Too soon and the people are not ready. We are not ready. The timing is off."

While Bani Sadr would never have been the savior of the Iranian people, his presence and the presence of those he appointed, all of whom were ideologically moderates, served to counterbalance the forces of right-wing religious fundamentalism. By July 1981, however, all hopes that he and his supporters would regain dominance were dashed. It was on a scorching afternoon that we all heard the news: President Bani Sadr had left the country. He had been flown out of Iran by airmen sympathetic to him. He had left his supporters, the nation, confused and without a leader. He had betrayed the nation, we all exclaimed. What a coward.

The regime spread rumors that he ran away dressed as a woman. This was done, of course, to discredit him even further. Dressed as a lowly woman, he fled the country to avoid prosecution for crimes against the revolution; crimes yet to be manufactured, of course.

Now, with the absence of his influence, the fanatics would have free, unfettered reign. His departure signaled the start of a renewed and intense wave of political repression and revenge killings. Ministers and politicians who had been political allies of Bani Sadr's were arrested and shot. Fundamentalist, conservative men took their places, and the noose tightened.

Bani Sadr was, at the time, the most significant symbol of moderate opposition to the religious fundamentalists. He was the face and voice of moderation. He had a following and political allies. He was not a leftist; he had no open ties to the Left, but he was someone with whom a coalition might be possible. His unseemly departure signaled to everyone that the opposition movement had lost. The forces of religious conservatism had won and their vengeance against all who opposed them would be horrific.

For Hadj, this was a difficult time. It was not so much that he personally had lost hope. It was more that the departure of Bani Sadr created a rift within his own political organization, between those who believed that the time for armed insurrection had now come and those who, like Hadj, felt that there was not enough popular support, there was not sufficient discontent among the majority of people, and therefore there would not be the popular support necessary to successfully overthrow the new ruling elite.

Of course, it is well documented that the 1979 revolution had not been a bloodless affair. Shah sympathizers and political allies were routinely executed. Armed national guardsmen and police shot into crowds of unarmed demonstrators, killing masses of them. There was blood. And, central to all of that was the power of the pulpit, the speeches calling for resistance made each Friday at prayer gatherings in every major city throughout the country. The religious Right had captured the hearts and minds of the people. And so, changing those minds and touching those hearts would require a lot more than rousing the rabble with fliers.

The next revolution would be a bloody civil war, we knew. Armies would form, alliances would be made. The "Party of God" would not go down quietly. They would call on their followers to sacrifice themselves as martyrs to the cause. Families would be torn apart as brother would turn against brother. Cities would be destroyed, roads bombed.

Hadj was no fancy political theorist. He was a people-person, whose greatest gift was his ability to connect with folks. He knew how to listen to people, and after months and months working in the heat of his south Tehran factory, lunching with the workingmen, and listening to them talk about the war, the country, the leaders, he knew the time for armed rebellion and civil war had not yet come. The people were not ready; his organization was not ready.

By late 1981 the political vacuum created by Bani Sadr's departure caused the regime to make decisive moves to finish off any hint of rebellion. Masses of young followers of left-leaning Muslim organizations and former pro-Soviet "urban guerilla" groups were rounded up, riddled with bullets, and thrown into mass graves. Periodically, the bodies would be saved for relatives, who would be charged per bullet hole for the privilege of retrieving an executed loved one.

Women were routinely gang raped prior to their summary executions. That an unmarried, nonvirgin cannot get into heaven was the stated justification. Young women and men were tortured, using the same horrific and cruel techniques used during the Shah's time; most probably using the very same torture devices I saw during my tour of the Central Prison soon after the revolution, when my idealism was at its peak.

This sickening wave of repression and murder shocked us all. And, at its height in January of 1982, a group of brave but misguided souls formerly closely affiliated with Hadj's group conducted an ill-conceived and disastrous armed uprising in the Caspian Seaside town of Amol. They called themselves *Sarbedaran-e Jangal*. *Sarbedaran* translated to "head in the noose," and *Jangal* means "forrest" or "woods," as the north of Iran was known for its lush greenery. With knowledge of the risks, their "heads in the noose," this band of 100 to 250 souls thought they would inspire an armed uprising against the Khomeini regime. They did not.

Hadj, along with the majority of his comrades, strongly opposed the action. It was ill-planned and executed, and it placed everyone at great risk. The plan had caused a great and irreparable divide in the leadership of Hadj's organization with the minority moving north to implement their poorly devised and tragic plan. For those who remained, opposed, the failure of the January uprising gave rise to heightened dangers. The organizations leadership went into hiding in safe houses throughout the country, conflicted but resisting any desire to flee the country they loved so much.

The impact on rank-and-file organizers, like Hadj, was palpable. More care would now need to be taken to appear "normal" and "disengaged" in politics. Now was the time to stop organizing and blend into the daily pattern of life.

"They did not trust the people," he would say, shaking his lowered head. "They thought they needed to do this *for* the people. Without the people, we will fail," he stated matter-of-factly.

"What will happen now?" I asked.

"It is now more dangerous for us. We need to lay low. I think we need to be very, very careful."

His words were, of course, prophetic.

CHAPTER 23

A BREAK FROM THE HEARTBREAK

The otherwise dark and repressive times we faced in 1981 were punctuated with parties and family outings. We left town one hot, smoggy, oppressive day in August, for the *Shomal* in the north and the Caspian Sea. Crammed into cars, the family caravanned out of Tehran, headed into the countryside and beyond. The road north is gorgeous. For people who believe the Middle East is one big desert complete with wandering camels, think again. For the record, I did not see one camel the entire time I was there. I am sure the roaming tribes of the southeast still use them. I didn't travel there, but there were no camels transporting people around in Tehran.

The landscape changes as you head north from Tehran, up through the mountains, alongside the vast river, where homes are built up on stilts. They are wooden homes, built in and among the trees that were used to construct them. Women dressed in brightly colored clothes—something not seen in the dull, dour big city—worked in the fields. Carrying their children, they bent and pulled, bent and planted, bent and hoed.

The villages found along the road to the north boast small coffeehouses. With an advance okay, a foreign bride is allowed to enter. As usual, I caused quite a stir, but the looks were simply kind and curious. I was not, I suppose, the first foreigner they had seen, as the north was a preferred vacation spot for the well-to-do. I might have been, however, the first woman allowed into the coffeehouse. I kept my scarf on, head down, voice low.

"Look," Aghajune said, pointing at the group of colorful women working the field nearby. "Look. The women work, the men drink coffee, as it should be," He laughed. He loved to pull my chain. He loved to joke, his eyes sparkling.

Iranjune, hearing this, laughed and looked at me knowingly. We laughed.

The weather in the north was clear and cool. The Caspian Sea, a vast expanse of blue water, surprised me. Along the shoreline, fishermen and restaurants called out to tourists to stop and spend. This was the source of Iran's prized caviar, to the chagrin of the Russians. As the story goes, the sturgeon simply decided they wanted to live on the Iranian side of the Caspian Sea. This prompted an informal caviar war. The Russians felt their caviar was the best. The Iranians knew theirs was the best. I don't care much for fish eggs so I could never weigh in on that battle.

What astounded me, however, was the fact that Muslims will not eat the sturgeon. Sturgeon does not have scales. Muslims—in food prohibitions probably lifted from the Jews—may not eat scaleless fish, pork, and, of course, drink alcohol. I have no idea what they did with the remains of the tens of thousands of sturgeon taken from the sea and harvested for their eggs. I am pretty sure, however, some folks just gave the big thumbs-up to the prohibition, in that thumbs-up Iranian way.

After getting settled into the small summer home owned by my sister-in-law's family, Hadj and I ventured out to swim in the Caspian. I, of course, had to wear long pants, a head scarf, and my *roo pusht* overcoat. He, a Speedo.

It didn't take us long to find a boat to rent and a willing captain. It was really nothing more than a motorized rowboat, but it served our purpose. After negotiating the price, the captain informed us— using his best conspiratorial voice—that I, too, could swim in the sea.

"I will take you out very far," he said, looking around for informers. "I will stand watch. You can swim. You can swim without the hijab." Cool.

We spent a half hour traveling away from the dock. When it appeared we were the only boat around for miles, our captain gave Hadj the go-ahead. Hadj wasted no time, dropping his pants, and ripping off his shirt and shoes. He dove into the water.

"Shit!" he yelled. "I forgot. It's saltwater!"

Modesty overcame me, coupled with the fear that someone might be watching with a telescope. I jumped into the water fully clothed. Now clothes weigh a lot. I also weighed a lot because I was pregnant. It took no small amount of effort on my part for me to get out of my jeans, take off my overcoat, shoes, and scarf underwater. Thankfully, this time I was wearing my bathing suit under the clothes. Using the scarf, I tied the entire lot into a soggy bundle, and then tied the bundle around my waist. It was like swimming with a dead body on my back.

I'm from California. I am a swimmer. I am not weak. I can lift stuff. This, however, was a challenge, and, yes, the water was salty.

In our past, the biggest inland body of water we had ever experienced was Lake Tahoe, a beautiful freshwater lake filled with crisp, cold water. The Caspian Sea is dark and salty. I gave up after ten minutes, but I spent the next half hour trying to get my soggy pants and overcoat back on. I struggled to exhaustion. Finally, sensing I was about to go under for the last time, Hadj held me up while I re-dressed. He got back into the boat and helped our amused captain drag me back out of the water like a soggy whale. While the captain and I sat silently together, Hadj swam laps around the boat.

You might wonder why Hadj seemed so unhelpful, particularly in view of my delicate state. It was because he was absolutely convinced that his American bride could do anything. Anything.

During our first year of marriage, I got my dream job hauling meat for a small, family-owned company in Richmond, California. I had originally been hired as the overnight auditor to collect the daily sales receipts and set up the delivery routes for the next day. I would organize the invoices by route and by stops to ensure each driver's route was the most time-efficient. Drivers would start at the closest location, and work themselves around the state, finishing at the point farthest away point. They would then drive back to the plant on double time.

The owners of the company were wonderful employers. Every single person employed by them received exactly the same base wage, which by 1976 standards was generous. They paid Teamster wages, although we were not a union shop. They were a delight to work for.

The drivers, while paid the same base as the rest, worked twenty-three-hour shifts quite regularly. This resulted in straight time, overtime, and then double time. They made a ton of money. I, too, wanted to make a ton of money.

After working graveyard for a couple of months, I approached the dock foreman one afternoon, having heard of an opening for a driver. It amused him. The company had never had a woman driver. He led me into the refrigerated warehouse, walking to the rear. Stopping in front of a pallet covered with boxes of frozen meat, he pointed down.

"Lift it up," he pointed. "Put it here," he said, gesturing to the five-foot-tall racks next to me. I bent down, picked up the box, and deftly put it on the rack.

"Okay," I said. "Where's the heavy stuff?"

"That was a hundred pounds," he said, looking me over. "That's our heaviest case. You can start training next week."

Shaking his head, he walked out of the freezer and back to his office.

Lifting one single one-hundred-pound case is not a problem. Unloading eight tons, well, that's a little different. After my first month, when I would come home exhausted, smelling of dead animal, unable to lift my arms, I got into the swing of it. I made a lot of money. I developed huge arms and thighs. It was the best job I had ever had.

Hudj was completely amazed.

"Of course you can do it, Lisa*Khanuum*," he said. "What made you think you couldn't?" (It is a bitch being married to a feminist at times.)

The absurdity of having to wear clothes to swim was almost too much. Women were on the beach, frolicking in the waves, with forty pounds of soggy outerwear dragging them under with each cycle. There had to be another way, and I soon discovered there was.

Apparently, in deference to the fairer sex and most likely to keep them out of the sea, the authorities had commandeered a large, formerly public, saltwater pool located adjacent to the sea. The pool was on the roof of the complex and thus obscured from the prying eyes of lascivious men by sheet upon sheet of black fabric, forming a modesty barrier.

I abandoned Hadj to the sea and hit the pool. There was no need for bathing suits here and I opted not to wear one. Women swam with enthusiasm in all sorts of underwear. The dreaded granny panties that had let me down in Tehran figured prominently in this setting. I shed my coverings and dove in. The water was warm, salty, and invigorating. I could really swim here. I impressed the girls with my breast stroke. I did a couple of laps and settled in, floating on the water, pregnant belly exposed to the world.

I was of course the object of much curiosity. There were no other foreign women in the pool, presumably because by that time few remained in the country or because they simply chose to stay on dry land.

I swam in the saltwater pool almost every day during that trip to the Caspian. I enjoyed the relaxed camaraderie of the women in the pool, particularly as I began to recognize faces. I enjoyed the communion with women, without needing to preen or pose or worry.

Hadj and I would take day drives, often just by ourselves. We drove to the Bacu region, which lies on the very southern rim of the former Soviet Union on Iran's northwestern border. We took the road along the Caspian until we could go no further and still be on Iranian soil. We drove to the border of Iran and the Soviet Union.

The border surprised me. There was a hut of sorts. There was a barrier. There appeared, however, to be no one manning it. I got out of the car and ran toward the border. I peered into the hut ready to find a sleeping guard of some kind, smile, and present myself as the American bride tourist that I was. Hadj, ever cautious and far more reserved, held back, calling out to me to stop running. The hut was empty. There was no one around. The coast was clear. I straddled the border—that imaginary line between countries. I hopped into the Soviet Union, I hopped back, all the while yelling: "Look...Soviet Union...Iran...Soviet Union...Iran!" He was not amused.

"Stop worrying," I yelled back at him from the Soviet side. "Like who would care?"

Bulletproof. That's what I thought I was. Bulletproof.

So I can now say I have been to the Soviet Union, via a deserted road in Bacu. It was no tourist haven, mind you. The towns in that region were dark and dull, industrial and depressing. But, hey, I was there.

As we drove down from the north through the villages and along the river, meandering back to the gray and the haze of Tehran, we felt renewed. I was ready to return to the slow, almost painful, pace of life punctuated with news of tragedy and upheaval.

CHAPTER 24
NOT JUST CHEESE

As much as I wanted to fit in, I was always just slightly outside the norm. I now felt keenly that detachment that Hadj had felt all of those years while living in California. My efforts to make Iranian food were met with nods and sympathetic smiles. It was never quite right. It always had an American twist to it. Over time I gave into it and decided my new culinary mission was to introduce the family to my American version of their delicacies.

I bought the flat, pliable *lavosh* cracker bread and used it as a makeshift tortilla. I was from California, after all, and thought I would show these folks my skill at producing the perfect burrito. It was a challenge, but I was up for it. It was no easy feat in those days, however, to come up with the rest of the ingredients for my own personal twist on a California favorite.

It is easy to take food for granted in the United States, particularly in California. We have an enormous variety of fruits and vegetables available to us all year-round. Our supermarkets offer a vast assortment of choices. We can buy organic produce, locally grown produce, and produce imported from thousands of miles away. Should we run out of an ingredient, we just send someone to the store to pick it up.

When we lived in California and visited the homes of Iranian friends, their dining tables would be covered with massive trays of fruits—oranges and plums, grapes, pears and apples. Mounds of small cucumbers piled neatly on silver platters would greet us. Our hostess would pick out the most attractive specimens of each manner of fruit, place them carefully on a small plate, and hand it to us. We would be given small knives for peeling the oranges or taking the skin off the cucumbers. It was slightly formal, but an essential part of the ritual of hosting guests.

Our Iranian student friends would, as they strolled the streets of Berkeley, always find themselves stopping to pick the plums and apricots that filled the trees along the way. Hanging abandoned and unloved, the fruit was apparently there for their pleasure. They would stand below the trees filling their mouths and expressing their amazement at the unclaimed bounty.

Like many Americans, I assumed that this abundance was present everywhere, that everyone had such constant access to food. After all, I thought, there must be supermarkets everywhere. I was wrong of course. When I moved to Iran, I was astounded at the lack of variety and availability. The marketplace always reflected the season and the economy. During the winter months, citrus was available, but it was imported and expensive. I would buy a bag of grapefruit and ration them out one a day until they were gone. I put myself on a grapefruit schedule.

I am sure that if I had had enough time and had been more adventurous, I could have scoured Tehran in search of other vegetables. I didn't. I made do. I used what I had and became creative with it. Periodically, however, I would venture out to the neighborhoods where the Armenian Christians lived, in search of some exotic component—like pineapple or soy sauce. It was a scavenger hunt of sorts. I would go from shop to shop, entering each one, waiting my turn. When the shopkeeper would deign to acknowledge me, I would ask in a low voice, if he had the item. It was as if I were purchasing contraband.

"Do you have pineapple?" I would ask conspiratorially, eyes darting about the shop.

"Are you American?" the shopkeeper queried.

"Yes."

He would then wait for the other patron to leave, and once we were alone, he would go to some special, secret place, and return with one dusty can of pineapple. I felt like a drug addict getting a fix. He would hand it to me, and I would pay some ridiculously exorbitant price for the can. I cannot describe the elation I felt after the transaction. It was invigorating and exhilarating at the same time.

I loved those Armenians. They made and sold wine and vodka on the black market. They had coffee—real coffee—the nectar of the gods. Hadj and I were coffee addicts. It was, of course, de rigueur for revolutionaries in Berkeley to be addicted to coffee. We would spend hours in coffee shops. Worse, we were actually coffee snobs. We knew what we liked and how we liked it prepared. We scorned Folgers and the like in favor of fresh-roast, freshly ground coffee. I had lovingly transported a Melitta drip coffeepot—the glass type with the wooden collar. It required filters, which I brought with me by the dozen.

I would travel to the center of Tehran to a huge, modern public coffeehouse where women and men would sit and drink coffee and tea, eat cakes, and chat. It was owned by Armenians, and it was open for a while, despite the pressures of the Hezbollah to ban coffee entirely. Coffee was not *naj jess* or religiously forbidden like pork, it was merely discouraged.

This coffeehouse reminded me of restaurants in the United States, as it was intended to do. Its large glass picture windows framed the busy street outside. Upon entering, a long, lighted counter containing pastries and sweets flanked the wall to the right. Formica-covered tables that looked like they had seen better days were arranged in long rows, four or so tables to a row. Men and women sat clustered around the tables, plastic bags containing the day's shopping lay on the floor.

The smell of freshly ground coffee assaulted the senses the minute the door opened. It was the smell of heaven, the smell of home—of laughter and chatter into the night, of plans being made, of capers being hatched. It was at once familiar and comforting. Ah, coffee.

Normally, customers could not buy coffee beans directly from the proprietor. Not knowing this, I asked our waiter if I could buy a pound of coffee. He looked at me, and it was clear that he had no idea what I was trying to say. He then hurried off, without bothering to answer. He returned shortly with a small, nervous-looking man with gray hair and a stubbled face.

"What is it you want?" he asked me in halting English.

"I want coffee beans," I replied. "Beans ground for Melitta."

Strangely, it never occurred to me that the proprietor would have no idea what a Melitta was. I just assumed all men who lived in the world of coffee knew every single method, accoutrement, and accessory relating to coffee worldwide.

"What is that?" he asked.

"I need to have the beans ground," I simplified.

"We do not sell beans."

"Can't you make an exception for me? I am an American friend."

I was not above begging. I was certainly not above playing any card I could to get those beans.

"Please?" I said, smiling at him, imploring him. "I will never tell where I got them from."

"It will be expensive," he said. I didn't really care.

I ended up spending the equivalent of one hundred dollars on that pound of coffee beans, and it was worth every penny. I guarded my coffee as if it were gold, allowing myself one cup each morning. I never made more than I needed. I never brought it out to share with the family. I was a selfish hoarder. I was an addict unwilling to share my stuff with anyone else.

I can live without a lot of things, but cheese is not one of them. Iranians mostly eat feta cheese. Periodically, they will come upon a package of processed cheese slices—the kind that are wrapped in plastic—and add that to a food. It is rare. None of the traditional foods incorporate cheese. My American friends and I would search up and down the boulevards of Tehran in search of that one Italian restaurant that had real, honest-to-God cheese in the food. We found one. It was heaven.

When a recipe called for cheese, the restaurants would use a processed-cheese-like item. It was a source of constant disappointment. I did not eat out often, but the search for real cheese kept me wandering the streets. I yearned for cheese. It created in me deep and ever-present hunger pangs. Without cheese, my life was empty and meaningless.

As luck would have it, Hadj's sister lived in Switzerland, the land of cheese. It was with breathless anticipation and unabashed joy that I received my first care package of cheese from her. She had sent us a one-kilo box containing a variety of cheeses. As it took days for the box to arrive, she had chosen hard, young cheeses that would age slowly. While most Americans keep their cheese refrigerated, Europeans do not. Cheese is placed on a board, covered with a dome of glass, and left to age at room temperature. Since the Europeans tend to shop daily, as the cheese is consumed, it is quickly replaced. Thus our box of cheese would arrive aged to perfection. And I would weep upon its arrival. Seriously.

Prior to being pregnant with Kian, I would create my own little cocktail hour by removing the bootleg vodka I had purchased from the Armenian up the street from its hiding place and mixing it with the juice of a freshly squeezed orange, if we had any. I would then carefully cut four or five slices of the beloved cheese and arrange them artistically on a small tray. I would cut pieces of cracker bread into small squares, preferably a piece that was slightly stale and crispy.

Having created this little tableau for myself, I would retire to the terrace as the sun set, sitting and listening to the call to prayer float on the breeze around me. It was sublime.

In 2015 I visited Hadj's sister in Switzerland with my sons. We had not seen each other in many years. She brought out the old photographs of Hadj and me, taken on our way to Iran in 1979 and remarked how our youngest son, Kassra, with his beard and his grin, reminded her of Hadj in his youth.

We had never actually discussed it before and she did not recall sending me the cheese. When I shared with her how overjoyed I was to receive her gift, she was surprised by its impact.

"There was a minute there when getting that cheese felt like it was saving my life," I told her plainly.

"It was just cheese."

CHAPTER 25
ALONE, BUT NOT LONELY

It's traditional in Iran for the entire family to come to the woman's bedside during labor. They come to wait, bringing food and drink, while the *laboree*—fully dressed in fancy nightwear—writhes around and entertains her guests.

Some months earlier, we had gone to visit my husband's niece while she was in labor in the hospital. Her room was filled with flowers and relations. Her mother had changed the standard-issue hospital bed linens and replaced them with a beautiful lace coverlet. She had on makeup. She was supposed to be our hostess. I was horrified. I walked out of that room vowing that should I ever become pregnant, I would not allow anyone to be in my room while I was in labor. I assumed I would be in labor for hours and hours. I planned on looking like crap the entire time and sweating profusely.

On the day of Kian's birth, a snowy day in January 1982, I decided to make sure the Mercedes was in good working order. My mother had reminded me on the phone that "Radcliffe women do not feel pain. If you wait for it to hurt, it will be too late." Thanks, Mom!

Hadj didn't feel much like driving that day, so I slid in behind the wheel of the Mercedes and backed it out onto the street. Our plan was simple: We would drive down to Mossadegh Avenue, make a turn, and drive back up to the house. We would spend maybe half an hour in the car. We just wanted to make sure the battery was charged, and it was ready and able to transport me to the hospital when the time was right.

As I turned right onto Mossadegh Avenue, traffic seemed manageable and I felt confident. I had been having false labor pains for weeks and figured we were getting close. This was my first baby. I had attended no childbirth classes. I had only just finished the book by the lovely British midwife. I decided that I would just sing if I felt stressed. Show tunes really work to alleviate tension for me.

As I slowed to make the right turn, the Mercedes was hit violently from behind. I pulled to a stop with a small truck still kissing my rear fender. I looked frantically at Hadi and he at me. Thankfully I was wearing a seat belt, slung low across my belly. I was fine.

"What do we do now?" I asked.

"We make sure they admit it was their fault and get money from them. We need to get them to pay for the damage. We want to make it quick. We don't want the police involved."

"Well," I laughed, "wait till they get a load of me. They just ran into a pregnant woman. If that doesn't make them feel guilty, nothing will."

I opened my door; and with great dramatic flourish, slid out from behind the wheel. Standing and facing the truck, holding my belly, I glared at the offending driver. There you go, I thought. Take a look at what you just hit.

Slowly his passenger-side door opened, and out stepped a small woman holding something in her arms. She was cradling a newborn.

"Shit. Trumped by a newborn. They win," I hissed.

Like many developing countries, the police can and do take bribes in Iran. When the police arrive after an accident, the cost to get out of the mess can increase exponentially. It would be better, Hadj explained, if we just took care of this ourselves. It seemed like a good idea to me.

We spent the greater part of the rest of the day following the people with the newborn who had rear-ended us to their home, where we sat politely on the floor of their lounge, as they brought us tea and treats. There was a lot of over-the-top politeness or *tarof*-ing going on. By this time, my back was killing me and I found it almost impossible to sit modestly and demurely on their floor. I kept whispering to Hadj to get to the point.

One does not just "get to the point," ever, in Iran. Being direct is considered rude. Business meetings can take hours. One must float around the topic in an ever-decreasing spiral downward, until finally, slowly, the point is raised. We were there to get money from these people to fix my father-in-law's precious Mercedes. We needed them to pay, but we could not pressure them.

Moreover, they did not appear wealthy. Their extended family lived together in a traditional one-story home. They seemed to take great pains to show us how many little mouths they had to feed, their humble home, their economic woes. We were sympathetic, but we needed the cash to fix the car. Eventually—after an eternity of polite chit-chat—we agreed on a price and a repair shop.

By the time we left their home, I was starving. We hit up a nearby *chelow kebab* restaurant for a meal of delicious kebabs and rice. I ate everything in sight. I felt strangely anxious and excited. We ran into some friends at the restaurant and joined them. It was a festive event as I stuffed the delicious meat and rice into my mouth. Sated and somewhat relaxed, we returned home. An hour later my water broke.

Getting to the hospital was an event. Hadj ran next door to alert his sister. My nephew Ali appeared, camera in hand. Pictures were taken of me midcontraction, standing in the backyard ready to go, flashing a *V* for victory. Two of my sisters-in-law were accompanying us to the hospital for moral support. Hadj, the sisters, and I crammed ourselves into the Mercedes, and off we went to the hospital.

The first five minutes of travel time were fine, but my contractions were coming fast and strong. I had, of course, no idea what to expect, but I intuitively felt it was all happening too fast. We arrived at the new, private hospital to find the elevator broken. I walked up the five flights of stairs, stopping periodically to breathe. Within minutes of my arrival, our son was born. There was little fuss or pain. I did, however, regale the delivery room with my rousing rendition of "Oklahoma!" I sang because my British Lamaze book told me to do what works for me. Singing loudly seemed to work.

Kian was born at 7:24 p m on cold January night.

Following his birth, I was wheeled alone and without my new son into a recovery room shared with two other women. It was apparently the "non-Farsi" room, as my roommates were a Zoroastrian and an Azerbaijani. Periodically throughout the two-day stay at the hospital, the nurses would bring in small tours of potential patients and point me out as "our American, who sings when she gives birth and did so in just forty-five minutes." It was my claim to fame.

Zoroastrianism dates back to pre-Christian, pre-Muslim times, and it was the primary religion in Iran centuries before. It is a religion based on the premise of good versus evil. There were very, very few left practicing by the winter of 1982, and currently the largest concentration lives in Pakistan. Zoroastrians' symbol can be seen throughout Iran as the square-helmeted head of a man on top of a span of eagle's wings. My mother-in-law told me they made the best electricians.

Azerbaijani people speak Turkish and originate from that northern area shared with Soviet Azerbaijan. The Farsi majority— the "real" Persians—tend to look down on the Azerbaijani. The prejudice is insidious and subtle. But it was there.

My husband, to his complete and utter dismay, missed the birth. Hadj had stepped out of the room to check on his sisters. Everyone, including me, thought I would be in the delivery room for hours. This would not be the case. Our son took forty-five minutes from doorstep to doorstep to enter the world. Hadj met his son as the nurses were bringing him out to take him to the newborn nursery.

My sisters-in-law—mindful of my wishes—went home with Hadj. I was alone, and alone I stayed…for days. The next day no one came to see me. No one brought me food. No one brought me flowers—no one, nada, zilch. I was completely alone. Later that day the nurses brought in my baby.

You might think my in-laws and husband were a heartless group, abandoning me in a strange hospital after the birth of a beloved male heir. Nothing could be further from the truth.

My in-laws really didn't know what to make of me. I was not like their daughters. I was tall and blue-eyed. I had a *damagh garuni* (an expensive nose)—short, snub, pug. Plastic surgeons in Iran charged a lot of money for my type of nose. I had met Hadj's parents in California before we had married. They liked the fact that I came from a "good family." During their brief stay in California, his parents, sisters, and their children rented a one-bedroom apartment and filled it with the smells of home.

My family had been invited to dinner. The food was delicious, but the meal was marked with long and often uncomfortable periods of silence. Hadj's dad stared blankly at my father. His mother smiled broadly, and attempted (bless her heart) to speak English with my mother. After much hand gesturing and nodding, a conversation of sorts was had, and a little bond formed. The food greased the skids. I had passed the test. The families declared us both worthy.

But my in-laws did not leave me alone in that hospital for days after I gave birth to Kian because they were mean. They did it to accommodate what I am sure they thought was my American way of having a child. They did it because it was what I had asked of them. They did it *for* me and not *to* me.

Hadj had been in exile for twenty years and he had forgotten some of the traditions. Or perhaps he just didn't know. So when Hadj and I visited our niece at the hospital while she was writhing around in heavy labor (and yet strangely with sufficient composure to offer us tea and cookies), he too was appalled. He had relayed my insistence that no one—repeat, no one—bug me at the hospital. Of course, everyone assumed he knew the hospital did not have a cafeteria. The reason for all those people being in that room with all that food was to make sure the new mommy was fed.

Thus, there I was— alone. Along and starving.

It was my roomies who came to my rescue. They took pity on me— the foreign woman. They displayed appropriate Iranian graciousness.

"How long for you? How much pain? So much!" One railed, looking at me with teary eyes.

"Ah…well…forty-five minutes," I replied.

"What? Forty-five hours! Oh, how terrible. You must tell your husband!"

"Ah, no…minutes…forty-five minutes…no real pain… very quick."

She eyed me suspiciously.

"Listen," she said to the lady to her left. "This American woman…only forty-five minutes and no pain. Do you believe it?"

"Oh no…I *still* have pain," moaned her neighbor. "Thirty-two hours…so much pain."

At that her husband and ten more relatives entered the room. This prompted another thirty minutes of wailing and whining, moaning and shrieking. I know she wanted her husband to know what he'd put her through. It felt a little staged to me, but he fell for it, and sat there looking guilty—yet sympathetic.

Plus, they had cookies. I was starving.

"You have no family?" my bed-neighbor asked. "Give her something. She has no one. No one is here. She is alone. Give the American something to eat."

"I have family," I managed to bark out, between bites. "I told them not to come."

"Why would you do that?" she asked in amazement. "Why do you want to be *tanha*?"

The word *tanha* in Farsi means both "alone" and "lonely." It was a word often used by others to describe me. Why are your reading *tanha*? Why do you sit here typing *tanha*? As many times as I responded I was just reading or just writing something, the response was the same: I was alone and thus apparently lonely.

But that night, after the momentous occasion of the birth of my son—I was indeed *tanha,* and it was all my fault.

I was allowed to stay at the hospital for two days and when Hadj came to take mc home, I told him about the food situation and the *tanha* comments. We laughed and laughed. We wrapped our beautiful son in the comforter my sister-in-law had made especially for that occasion and took him home.

CHAPTER 26
YOU'VE MADE A MISTAKE

The 1979 seizure of the US embassy was the single most fear-inspiring incident to hit the American public in decades. The Iranian students who took over the embassy not only violated the law, they violated American pride and sense of decency. The world stood up and took notice, and the foreign press descended upon Tehran to report. To make sense of it all, the issue had to be pared down to what the media believed was its lowest common denominator: us against them. They hate us; we should hate them.

Reporters would stand in front of Tehran University, filming nightly news segments by referring to the university as the "site of fervent anti-American hysteria." I recall standing next to just such a reporter with my two obviously American women friends, listening to him make this statement and knowing that my parents would be sitting at home, terrified for me, watching the broadcast. The message was decidedly wrong and I believed it was calculated to promote fear and controversy. Fear draws a crowd.

I can say with great certainty that the vast majority of the Iranian people did not hate the American people. They hated foreign intervention. They feared the imposition of Western values. Promoting misinformation served only to foment antagonism at home. It also promoted a general misconception that we American expats were at risk in Iran. This was simply not true.

Despite my somewhat skittish anxiety, I had only one experience the entire time I was in Iran when I believed I might fall victim to a criminal assault. Just one. In contrast, my Iranian friends in California were not treated so kindly. Iranian friends who were continuing their studies on college campuses around California were routinely threatened. Iranians were bullied and terrorized. One of my female friends was so abused by her American peers that she was approached by the president of her campus's Black Student Union (BSU) and offered protection. A BSU member would walk her to and from class every day, and escort her to her car at night. It was horrific.

I, however, only had one incident in which I felt threatened. I had hailed a cab up the main boulevard and was headed home. Taxis in Iran run north–south or east–west, picking up and dropping off fares, keeping the car completely full at all times. The streets were dark as a result of the blackout I felt it rather strange that I was the lone passenger in the taxi, but I chose to push the trepidation out of my mind. As we drove north, I gazed inattentively out the window.

I had told the driver very specifically, I was headed to *Tajrish*, a well-known square in the north of the city. It is also a landmark in a well-to-do neighborhood. To get there just involved driving uphill.

I came out of my reverie when I realized we were not going up. He had turned east, and we were heading out in the dark toward an industrial area of Tehran. It was an area populated by factories and warehouses. It was dark and isolated. It was not where I wanted to be driven.

I could see the driver's eyes as they darted from the road and back to the rearview mirror. I could see he was watching me watch him.

I had brought a standard-issue Swiss Army knife with me to Iran. I loved the knife and its various functions, all of which I had used on one occasion or another. This time its intended function would be to scare the crap out of the driver.

When I was delivering meat in California, the other truck drivers presented me with my own official meat hook. I was advised to put it in my belt and "pull it out and hold it up if they mess with you."

Shortly thereafter I had occasion to use it. I was accosted by a horny butcher in the back freezer. Women meat haulers were few and far between, and he had never seen a twentysomething-year-old one in a mini smock with steel-toed shoes. His interest thus piqued, he grabbed me in the freezer and pushed me up against the wall.

Without missing a beat, I pulled out my meat hook, placed its point up against the side of his neck and calmly, but firmly said to him, "If you ever touch me again, I will rip out your fucking throat."

Apparently, he believed me. He stepped back. Later, during a subsequent delivery, I heard him tell another driver that after seeing me throw off those hundred-pound cases of meat from the back of the truck, he was pretty sure I could take him. Word spread. They left me alone.

It was that same spontaneous reaction that caused me to pull out my trusty Swiss Army knife that night, open it up, and hold the blade high enough for the driver to see.

"We are going the wrong way," I said, flatly. "Turn north. This is not the way to Tajrish."

I could see I had startled him. He began to attempt to tell me I had made a mistake—that this *was* the way. I lifted the knife, pointing the blade at the back of his neck.

"*Shomah, esht abad car did* (You have made a mistake)," I said slowly, enunciating each and every syllable, deepening my voice to sound as menacing as I could.

Within minutes, he had turned back toward the main boulevard. I exited the car and, turning toward the open window, threw my money at him. I was shaking. I was pissed. But I was truly impressed with myself, I dared say. My Clint Eastwood demeanor had saved the day.

CHAPTER 27
GOING BACK TO CALI(FORNIA)

Almost immediately following Kian's birth in January 1982, I began my campaign to nag Hadj into returning to California for a brief visit with me to show off my parent's newest grandson. Aside from the growing political repression, I feared cholera season. I feared not having access to infant immunizations, as my pediatrician had told me that they were becoming more and more difficult to get into the country. I planned on having all of those done in California.

It was not an easy sell. Because I had no "need to know," Hadj did not immediately share with me the new level of danger in which he found himself following the ill-fated Amol uprising. While I understood that arrests and executions were being conducted in obscenely record numbers, I chose to ignore the events taking place outside our walled nest and focus on our new son.

Hadj told me that he was, of course, happy to have me take Kian to the US for his shots, but I would be by myself. We argued constantly about whether or not I could make the trip alone with an infant and Hadj, in his infuriating way, ever confident in my ability to do anything, assured me it would be just fine. It was maddening.

Again, the times were horrifying with daily reports of raids leading to mass executions. Propaganda-heavy "news" reports described the capture and arrest of dissidents. The government would not readily disclose the fact that these dissidents were subjected to the most inhumane torture and imprisonment. The regimes hid the fact that all of the old SAVAK secret police files were now in the hands of the new version, SAVAMA, and used for the same purposes: identify, surveil, and later arrest.

Individuals were routinely declared "enemies of the revolution," a sufficiently vague "crime" that would and did result in imprisonment or execution. I had always assumed that a file had been kept on Hadj by SAVAK and was simply transferred to SAVAMA. I had hoped that as long as he appeared to be keeping himself out of political activism, he would go untouched. I hoped that Hadj's almost obsessive habit of working deep undercover among the people in southern Tehran, actually building a factory and actually employing local workers, while gaining their respect as a good and fair businessman, had paid off. No one outside the organization, I prayed, knew about his secret meetings and his secret work as a committed activist. I believed that no one would be privy to his true activities other than the people who needed to know.

The horrors of the purge of opposition forced Hadj to significantly tone down his political work. The repressive political climate that encouraged neighbors to spy on neighbors cast a stifling cloud over the society as a whole. It was a dangerous time for activists and organizers in Iran. And I, naïve as I was and with that special arrogance found among young idealists, believed that these horrors would never touch our new little family. We were safe, I thought. We would now, for the time being, just live the life of suburban middle-class folks with a new baby.

While the political climate in January-February 1982 was intense, we continued to live outwardly appearing very quiet lives as a "small factory owner and his American bride." My constant insistence that Hadj get "time off" to accompany me to California must have been shared with his comrades as it was also around that same time that we had repeated visits from our old Berkeley friend, Ahmed.

Ahmed was someone Hadj had worked with in the Iranian student movement in Berkeley. Much like Hadj, he held various leadership positions in the Iranian student movement. While I had zero idea what he was doing in Iran at that time, I welcomed him into our house where we reminisced about our time in California.

He and his brother had been, for all intents and purposes, raised in the US. They had traveled to the Midwest as young teens and found themselves living on the farm of an American family whose father had befriended their father some years back.

"My first night there," he once told me, the first time we met while we sat drinking bad coffee at the local IHOP, "they made me get out of bed so they could use it for a sick calf." A broad smile covered his face, unobstructed by his huge, thick mustache.

He would regale me with funny stories about being the only foreigner in a very small, rural farming town. Having lived so long in the heartland, Ahmed had a very well-developed American sense of humor, which I found comforting and familiar.

But on that day in April, as he sat in our formal living room, a cigarette dangling from his mouth and a glass of tea perched on the arm of the chair, his demeanor was anything but amusing.

"Hadj," he intoned, deep furrows appearing across his forehead. "You cannot leave at this time."

"First," Hadj declared, "I haven't decided if I am going or not. But if I do, I am not planning on leaving for good," Hadj laughed, trying to put him at ease. "It would be for a month or so."

"Things are happening NOW! You cannot go NOW." His tone was dark and desperate. His demeanor severe and pleading.

"There are plans," he insinuated. "Things that we need you to do. You have your priorities mixed up. Lisa can take care of herself. You are vital to our movement."

Hadj had been around the political movement long enough to understand that playing the guilt card; that the suggestion that one would put one's own priorities ahead of the needs of the "movement," was a common method of persuasion.

"Look, it's only a few weeks" I interjected. "The world will not end if he goes with me for four weeks."

"Frankly, this is the best time. The production is over and we are putting the heaters on the market. Marketing is not my job. My other work," Hadj continued, lowering his voice, "can wait for a few weeks."

But Ahmed would not be deterred. He returned several times as our date of departure loomed, each time his mood darkened, his allegations of "self-interest" and "bad priorities" deepened. But his demands that Hadj stay could not hold up to my incessant nattering and nagging.

It took time and effort, but eventually I cajoled Hadj into agreeing to return briefly to California. We had planned on making the trip in July, but events over which he had no control intervened.

CHAPTER 28
CLOSING IN

By the early days of 1982, we suspected that our English-language institute, a place we thought was so secure and useful, was under surveillance. The presence of random bearded men loitering around the entrance had us spooked. Hadj did not know if we had called attention to ourselves with our comings and goings or if someone had seen our night visitors sneaking into the building in the wee hours. Perhaps, we opined, one of our neighbors had said something to someone who told someone. And they, in turn, told someone in the *Basij*. We had no way of knowing.

It was now early Summer of 1982 and the repressive fist of the fundamentalist right had come down hard and fast on the opposition. Having literally massacred thousands of young followers of the Mujahideen and other "leftist" organizations, the regime had turned its sights on groups they thought could conceivably organize any type of opposition, large or small.

In an abundance of caution and for everyone's safety, we decided to close the school and dismiss our teachers. It was time to scatter, to become reabsorbed into daily chores and shopping and work. Each teacher would return back to her life, trying to distance herself from us and slip back into an invisible routine.

Needing to make sure that every trace of any of us and the beloved mimeograph machine were swept from the rooms, we decided to drive down the hill to the five-story office building that housed our school. Holding our infant son in my arms and sliding into the backseat of the Mercedes, Hadj and I headed downtown toward the school building.

Traffic, as always, was horrific as Hadj weaved in and out between taxis, speeding cars and motorbikes. I sat back, clutching Kian firmly in my arms and bracing myself up against the backrest as we made the perilous trek toward the center of town.

As we pulled onto the street, miraculously finding a parking space directly in front of the door to our building, Hadj pretended to look for something on the front seat while hissing, "He's right there, in front of us, leaning up against the pole."

Trying to look without looking, I noticed the medium-height, dark man with the five-day beard. He was relaxed against the street sign on the corner, facing our car, and he openly watched as we exited the vehicle. He did not attempt to conceal himself. He was pointedly brazen and I was terrified.

Clinging to Kian, I quickly entered our building and made my way up the stairs to the fifth floor, with Hadj moving swiftly behind me. When we reached our floor, Hadj pressed past me to unlock the metal and glass doors leading into the suite of offices. Both of us were out of breath.

Suddenly the phone rang, with the shrill sound of each impatient ring cutting through the air. Startled, I lurched toward it, still cradling Kian, still breathless.

"*Allo,*" I answered, tentatively.

The voice on the other end was familiar. The accent unmistakable and American.

"Hey, salaam," she began. "I've been out of town. Heard something," she continued, cryptic and haltingly.

"You don't need to come to work today. It is *not* a good day," I replied, emphasizing "not" and hoping she would get the message. "We had some new people show up for lessons, but all they wanted to do was hang around outside and smoke," I continued, again hoping she would understand my message.

Our school had a phone, which we had always treated as being tapped. I believed that any phone vaguely associated with a foreigner such as myself was tapped. I had conversations with my family in California abruptly cut short with the line going dead on many occasions.

"Go *away,*" I implored, again emphasizing "away" and hoping the message got through.

The phone line went dead. Did she hang up? Or were we cut off? Panic set in and it became difficult to concentrate. Mind racing, I turned to Hadj. He had been listening to the exchange.

"Should I have said more? Should I have just said get the hell out of the country? Are they coming for us?" I asked Hadj, confused and in panic.

Hadj stood back from the window overlooking the street and pointed out the man dressed in a dark, dusty-gray jacket, who now sat in an old Mercedes across the street. He had been joined by another, and from the windows of our fifth-floor unit, we could see them leave the car from time to time and lean up against the mulberry trees lining our street, smoking, watching.

"Are we just paranoid?" I asked him, still not believing that this could be happening.

"I really don't know," he replied cautiously. "I don't know if it is me they are following or you."

We checked and double-checked the offices, making sure no scrap of paper or drop of mimeograph ink was found. We carefully erased the blackboards we often used for our "escape English" lessons, taking great pains to scribble over the old, faint traces of chalk and then erase again. We wanted to be sure not to give anyone any conceivable excuse to come after us.

We turned off the lights, locked the doors and, hoping to return someday, we headed home.

"After all," I announced to Hadj, "I am American. They wouldn't dare," my voice trailed off.

But they did.

CHAPTER 29
OUR AMERICAN FRIENDS

Only days after we had gone to close up our school, the loud buzz of our doorbell and the banging of metal against our metal front door interrupted my afternoon. I was alone at home, and thankfully Kian was asleep in the next room. I grabbed my head scarf off the coat hook, carefully covering my head before opening the door to find two men.

They were dressed in a similar fashion to the men who had placed themselves in the old Mercedes outside our school. In my panic, I could not tell if they were indeed the same two men. They did not identify themselves They showed me no official badge. They had no uniform. One of them carried an AK-47 casually slung over his shoulder. I assumed he had used the butt end of the weapon to knock on the door. He did not point it at me as others had done, and I prayed it was a good sign.

"*Khanuum* Azimi? (Mrs. Azimi)" one asked.

"Yes?" I replied, softly.

"Do you know Lisa Radcliffe?" he questioned, holding up a photo for my inspection. "This is her. Do you know her?"

The air left my body.

"Holy shit," I thought, mind racing. "They don't know that this is a picture of me."

Keeping my head down, I dared not make eye contact.

"I know her," I said.

"Where is she?" Oh my God. Oh my God. Oh my God! my brain screamed.

"She left. She went back to America. She is gone."

"When did she leave?" one demanded.

"Last week, I heard," I lied.

And then to my complete astonishment, having believed me, they turned and left. They did not say good-bye. They did not ask a single additional question. They simply concluded their business and, finding me completely uninteresting, they left.

I closed the door and collapsed onto the steps leading up to the foyer.

The photo that those two men showed me that afternoon was not a surveillance photo, taken secretly of me walking about town. It was a photo that I had seen before, a photo that had appeared on the front page of *Kayhan International*, a prominent daily newspaper, the previous year. In the photo, taken in December 1979, I am standing behind a podium, beige shawl covering my head, earnest expression on my face, and finger pointing out toward an unseen audience.

It was on that date in 1979 when my American women friends and I found ourselves in front of Tehran University watching the

Western television reporter open his story by describing it as "the site of fervent anti-American hostility." I could not control myself. Hearing those words, I loudly interrupted his filming and began arguing with him about his reporting bias in front of a growing crowd of students.

"My family will see this crap!" I shouted to him. "Do we look like we are in danger?" I screamed, pointing at my American friends.

He said nothing in response and retreated to his car. I had caused a scene. And, appreciating what they believed to be enthusiastic support for their cause, the students asked if we would join them for an impromptu seminar on how we believed the American public viewed the seizure of the embassy. They thought that we would have a better insight seeing that we straddled the line between being American and living with Iranians. We gladly agreed, but with the caveat that we were no experts.

The students ushered us into an empty lecture hall and, within minutes, over a thousand seats were filled. They provided a podium and a translator. And we then conducted an informal seminar.

It was during this seminar, at a point when I stood at the podium to answer questions, that the photo was taken and published on the anniversary of the revolution with the caption: "Even our American friends support our Revolution." Hadj laughed riotously when he first saw it. Irony at its best.

We were not laughing now.

"We have got to leave now," I announced curtly to Hadj, as he walked in the front door. "Now."

CHAPTER 30
PLAYING WITH PISTACHIOS

As we stood at the customs table in Tehran Airport in mid-June of 1982, I carried our four-month-old son in my arms. Our suitcases lay open in front of a uniformed inspector. He had our passports and was scrutinizing them, looking at them and then up at us.

"Stay here," he commanded, as he turned with our passports in hand and walked into the open office behind him. Leaning over a desk, we could see him conferring with another man in uniform. They looked at our passports; they looked at me; they looked at Hadj.

I drew Kian closer to me and tried to control my breathing.

"What is going on?" I whispered to Hadj.

"I don't know."

"What should I do?" I asked.

"Keep calm."

"Did they figure out it's me?"

"I can't tell."

The border agent returned and handed us back our passports without deigning to explain to us what the problem was. He then occupied himself with searching our bags. We were not out of the woods yet.

I had sewn five crisp one-hundred-dollar bills in the waistband of my husband's pants. I had placed my US passport and the US passport of our infant son, newly obtained through our friends at the Swiss consulate, in a Baggie inside his soiled diaper. A good Muslim will not touch baby poop. I was confident that no one would search there.

The money, however, worried me. As his fingers moved around the edge of the pants, I panicked. They had already been out looking for me. A man had appeared at our front door, with my photo in hand, asking for me. Now, here I was with my name plainly printed on my Iranian passport, baby in my arms, trying to leave the country. How is it they hadn't stopped us by now? Were they after Hadj instead?

The man standing in line next to me had placed a large bag of pistachios on the floor near my feet. As the agent's fingers approached the waistband of Hadj's pants, I quickly kicked out with my left foot while simultaneously pinching my infant on the leg. Kian wailed. The bag of pistachios hit the floor, spewing hundreds of the little round nuts across the ground. All hell broke loose. I feigned an apology, profusely begging my neighbor's pardon. The customs agent, clearly annoyed by the noise and confusion, handed us back our passports and summarily shooed us through and into the waiting area. We sat and waited, saying little to each other. We knew we were not safe yet. We were not on the plane and out of danger. They could, as they had before to other travelers, still take us off the plane minutes before take-off in a cruel maneuver specifically intended just to mess with us.

These were the men who dragged men and women before mock firing squads. These were men with no souls.

Even with the engines starting and the airplane moving down the runways; even after take-off, we did not feel entirely safe until the pilot announced we had left Iranian airspace. Upon hearing the words, "Ladies and gentlemen, we have now left Iranian airspace," every woman on the plane stood, as if choreographed. Looking defiantly around our seats, we took our scarves off our heads, and dropped them to the floor. One by one, scarves floated to the floor, in a spontaneous display of protest. I sat down and felt suddenly naked and exposed.

We traveled first to Switzerland to stay with Hadj's sister. His Green Card had expired and thus it was necessary for him to make the trek to the US Embassy in Bern to have it renewed. Two weeks later, we stepped off the plane at San Francisco International Airport to the smiles and hugs of my parents.

CHAPTER 31
SURVIVOR'S GUILT

While in the United States, communications with our family and friends in Iran was a carefully planned dance. We assumed, of course, that someone was always listening in on the phones. Family members involved in political activism knew to use public phones. But even that was problematic, as one had to go to a telephone exchange office to make a long-distance call. In response to this, we had agreed that certain code phrases would be used for calls to transmit information.

"Ali Reza just had a baby," she informed Hadj one evening in mid-July. This was the code for friends had been arrested.

"Was there a party?" Hadj asked, using that phrase to replace the question "how many?"

"Well, a lot. We went, too."

The air left his body as he willed himself to finish the "chat" with the expected banal banter

His heart sank. "We went, too." Hadj knew immediately what this meant. It meant that the caller's husband and many of his friends and comrades had been arrested. It was, he knew, a death sentence. And he was not there to save anyone.

"I should have stayed," he announced, turning to me, his face ashen and tears welling up in his eyes. "I should never have left. I could have done something. I could have helped them."

"Why did you talk me into leaving?" he demanded.

"There was nothing you could do. They would have arrested you, too. How would that have helped?" I pleaded. "How?"

We had been in California for a very short time when that call came in. The "comrade" who was so anxious for us to stay, Ahmed, had become an informant for the regime. We now knew why he was so adamant that Hadj stay.

He gave them names and addresses of the leadership of Hadj's organization. He gave them all up to the regime, including his own brother and sister-in-law. This was the man who had come to our home repeatedly, attempting to stop Hadj from leaving with Kian and me. He sat across from me. He drank my tea and wanted my husband to suffer torture and imprisonment and execution.

Targeting the leadership, the regime sought to sever the head from the body of Hadj's organization. The men and women arrested were the bravest of souls. They were selfless and committed to the honorable goal of a new, free, and democratic Iran. They were fathers and mothers, sisters and brothers, husbands and wives. They were young teachers or talented engineers. They had large, loving families who stood behind them, proudly, even at their own peril. They were the face of Iran's future and true martyrs to the cause of freedom.

The official line was that their actions were found to be "crimes against the revolution." The regime, wanting to appear justified, played out a mock trial on television. Nightline reported on it, actually suggesting that the trial was a sign of Iranian "due process" of law. It was, of course, in reality a circus produced only to shield the horrific abuses perpetrated on the opposition by those in power.

In late January 1983, after the conclusion of the judicial farce, they were taken to the north of Iran near the site of the rebellion, and lined up in front of a mass grave, where they were unceremoniously shot. As punishment, their families were denied the right to retrieve their bodies. No proper burial having been done, no public grief could be displayed.

A few days later our phone rang again in the middle of the night.

"They have killed them. They are dead," the voice on the phone announced and then abruptly hung up.

Hadj, still holding the phone receiver to his head slid down the wall into a heap on the floor.

We knew our friends could not escape death. We knew they had suffered torture and degradation. We even saw them featured in a "Nightline" segment, sitting stoically behind a long desk at a "trial" manufactured by the regime as an example of "justice." But for Hadj, hearing the words made it overwhelmingly real. His grief was indescribable, his sadness heartbreaking. The fallout from that single phone call clouded our lives for years.

Night after night, for months, he would sit in the dark, tears streaming down his face. They were his brothers and sisters. They were his family. He had spent countless hours arguing, discussing, analyzing, singing and eating with them. Our brother-in-law, among the dead, was a brilliant man lost too soon.

Playing the events over and over in his head, Hadj was haunted by the certainty that he was allowed to pass through customs on that summer day in 1982 because and only because had he been arrested, the news would have spread and the other activists would have fled or gone into hiding. Considering the timing of the event and the prior attempts to keep him from leaving, Hadj's belief was grounded in reality.

If truth be told, I made him leave Iran. I nagged him mercilessly. I cajoled. I wept. He had to go with me. They were following him, us. They came for me. I couldn't travel halfway around the world with an infant. He needed to be there. He caved in finally—as I knew he would—and we left. We left and we lived. They did not.

In the cold light of day, our rational minds knew we were not saviors. We could not save the world. I knew that if Hadj had stayed in Tehran, he would have been shot and buried along with his comrades. He could not, however, accept this truth.

"It is all your fault," he would tell me, tears streaming down his face. "It is all your fault. You made me leave. You made me come here. You did this."

CHAPTER 32
THE END OF AN ERA

Make no mistake, "survivor's guilt" is real and Hadj could not escape its grip on him. He actually believed his survival was an act of cowardice. He had lived and others had not. He could not shake the pain and disappointment, no matter how hard he tried. Everything he had worked for, all of his efforts to build coalitions and support for his people, was over. The Iranian Students Associated was disbanded and impotent, its leaders unceremoniously thrown into an open grave.

Feeling lost and without purpose, he sunk into a deep and almost debilitating depression.

But, we had a new baby, only the clothes on our backs and a life to get back to living. So we shoved our grief deep inside and started to rebuild a life in California.

At that point, the atmosphere in California was decidedly anti-Iranian. Despite its reputation as a left-leaning haven, the unrelenting campaign to color all Iranian's as anti-American, appeared to have succeeded.

I had no problem finding a job with a women's clinic with the foresight to provide an on-sight daycare facility for staff children. Hadj, on the other hand, could not cut a break. Former employers shut the door on him; new, prospective employers inevitably figured out his country of origin.

"I'm gonna just start telling these guys I'm Italian," he laughed.

It was pointless.

"I am going to open a business," Hadj announced, one day with great flourish.

"Okay, what kind?" I asked.

"I don't know."

In Iran, the merchant class or "bazaari'i" class are generally rich, conservative and religious. Their "store fronts" are deceptive, as they appear to the uninformed to be small, crowded storefront shops. They are not. They are simply the public face of the enterprise and supported by large warehouses located elsewhere.

And so, each morning I would hustle off to work with our baby son, Kian, while Hadj threw himself into what he would come to see as his new campaign to figure out what type of businessman he wanted to become. It was just the sort of diversion he needed.

Needing more income, I left the women's clinic and lied my way into a job as the executive assistant to a senior bank executive. I could not type, but I knew how to get things done. The executive was short of both stature and patience: He had hired and fired six of my predecessors during the preceding eight weeks. He was brash and rude and inappropriate on so many levels. He did not scare me. I had, after all, looked down the barrel of an AK47.

During Hadj's journey to figure out what kind of businessman he wanted to be, we looked at bars and restaurants and we investigated franchises. We finally settled on opening a delicatessen because, and this is true, it would allow us to have unfettered access to coffee.

We had absolutely no idea how to go about opening a business, and yet Hadj had decided to move forward and risk failure. This meant he had to find a location, build it out, get permits and plans approved.

To do this, he needed help, so he conscripted my best friend, Heather, to serve as his "day wife/driver/secretary." Every day, Heather would appear at our apartment door, ready to chauffeur Hadj from office to office, allow him to give her "orders," all the while he ignored all of her excellent advise.

I mean, after all, Heather had an MBA. Hadj, however, had a joyful enthusiasm and a bossy demeanor. Heather would give good and solid advice to Hadj, which he would promptly and charmingly ignore. She became, of course, Heather*khanuum* and would remain so until he died.

Heather, who was briefly between jobs and low on cash, would show up at our home to eat *Addas pollo*, a rice and lentil dish made with dates and ground meat and savory spices. To this day, a good plate of it will make Heather tear up.

We owned the deli for just enough time to have two more beautiful sons and watch our marriage slowly implode.

Our son Kaveh appeared in 1984, while our enthusiasm for our new enterprise soared. Our third son, Kassra, was born in 1986, just as we were investigating our bankruptcy options.

It was a time of extreme personal and financial stress for both of us. Hadj and I had come together to serve alongside each other as soldiers in a cause. We had watched horrors occur and we had experienced several moments of abject terror. These things happened to us, binding us closer together.

But the execution of friends, family and comrades left Hadj feeling powerless and defeated. His depression made him withdrawn and morbid and uncommunicative. For my part, I was emotionally ill equipped to just grow up and help him deal with his pain.

We closed our business and I filed for divorce.

. . .

Hadj continued to call me every day after our divorce. It was a pattern that started early on in the proceedings, as we both felt compelled to brag about our beautiful boys to each other on a regular basis.

At first, my responses were short and rude. I felt he was trying to "control me" because, of course, as I was known to exclaim "he was not the boss of me." Clearly, I did not understand until much later that this was not control, but rather respect and affection.

Each and every time he sought my counsel was an act of affection. Asking me, persuading me, this was the vocabulary of Hadj's love and affection. This was the only way he knew how to communicate these feelings to me. This was our bond and we continued to share it for the next twenty years.

After a time, I came to understand our special and unique relationship. We had lived in separate homes, in separate cities, and maintained a bond of loyalty and affection that persisted. Any anger or disappointment or resentment we had directed toward each other had long faded. Our memories of the conflict and emotional distance that had divided us were replaced with the deep and lasting bonds of respect.

Our youngest son, Kassra, came home one day during his first week in kindergarten and announced breathlessly and with great conspiratorial flourish that "Johnny Smith's mommy and daddy live in the same home!"

He had been born into our divorce, and it was all he knew. As he aged, like his brothers, he came to understand the unconditional bond of love between his father and me, the unbreakable connection Hadj and I had created in love, through our shared past.

"I get it now," he declared, "you and dad are meant to be best friends, but not married people."

Yes.

CHAPTER 33
OLDEST LIVING FRIEND

"Lisa*june*, you are now my oldest living friend," Hadj announced to me over the phone one day, following the news that one of the old guards had died of addiction and heartbreak. "We must never fight again."

In his short, declarative way, Hadj had summarily stopped all conflict between us. We were bound together for life. We could not escape the fact that we belonged to a small, elite club of people who had experienced history and seen the object of our hopes evolve into a sad mutation of our aspirations. Hadj was trapped in California and, once again, he could not return to his country, his homeland, his people.

We parented our sons together as friends, collaboratively. We attended every single school event and game together. Our sons' teachers often didn't know we were divorced and were surprised to discover we had, by then, actually been divorced longer than we had been married. Hadj would attend basketball games, watching with the appropriate level of paternal pride as one or another of our sons did something we believed was spectacular on the court.

After we separated and while I went to law school, Hadj watched the children. He lived in a studio apartment so our boys could have the use of most of his income. As a divorce lawyer myself, I know how unusually generous that was. But, of course, Hadj was unusually generous. He was the kindest man I have ever known.

We both hoped to instill in our children a strong sense of family and community. They were encouraged to follow their passions and to make a difference in the world. Each, in his own way, has done so.

Hadj would routinely take the boys to the poorest sections of Oakland or San Francisco to make sure they knew how many people lived in scarcity. He would take them to serve Thanksgiving dinners to the poor and to volunteer at the Special Olympics.

I was so young when we married. It all seemed like a wonderful adventure. I cannot say that I was truly, fully in love with Hadj when I married him. I was too young to know what that meant. But I was besotted. Over time, our love and respect for each other deepened profoundly and manifested through our wonderful children. Our relationship transformed into a warm and easy friendship.

On September 13, 2003, I received a call from Hadj. It was the middle of the day and his voice on the line immediately annoyed me. After our divorce, I had gone to law school and became a family law attorney, and I had a client meeting to get to.

"What?" I demanded impatiently. "I have a client coming in. What is it?"

"I have lung cancer."

I felt the air leave my body.

"What? How? That's insane!" I yelled into the phone. "You don't smoke. You work out two hours a day. You have the body of a 30-year-old!"

Anger rose in my throat like a toxic bile.

"This has got to be a mistake," I whined.

But, it was no mistake. Hadj, who had lived his entire adult life as a non-smoking athlete; who had not eaten meat in two decades; who worked out two hours a day, had developed a rare form of lung cancer. And no one caught it because he looked just too damned healthy to be sick.

He was not much of a complainer, but had called me weeks before to warn me that he thought something might be wrong. I didn't believe it and found myself being almost dismissive.

"Go to the doctor. Make them take x-rays," I responded curtly. "It's probably nothing".

But by the time that Hadj's doctors decided to respond to his complaints, the cancer had spread to his bones. He was 63 years old. He was a fighter. He would not take this laying down. He would battle to the very, very end.

As Hadj willed it to be so, for the next two years he fought. His lung tumors were reduced to almost nothing, thanks to an experimental medication that showed great promise with Japanese women. We would often joke that underneath his strong, Persian exterior, one found a healthy Japanese woman.

"I am not going anywhere."

I had to believe him. His boys had to believe him. He was, after all, a force of nature; a persuader. He was a fighter. He had flaws and fears, but he would not leave us passively.

He fought hard, and was even in remission for two years, but the cancer ultimately won and on September 24, 2005 at around noon, Hadj died surrounded by his family.

I spoke to Hadj nearly every day for thirty years until the day he died.

He was a truly remarkable man and has left a legacy of three remarkable young men to follow their passions.

Hundreds of people came to his memorial, held on a cool October afternoon in 2005. They came to pay their respects, to honor, and to mourn. The meeting hall was full, forcing latecomers to stand outside. The crowd extended to the parking lot and up onto the lawn beyond. Poems were read and speeches were given in his honor. It was an event he would have loved to organize. It was fitting.

The following day we took his ashes to the cliffs near our beloved Fort Cronkhite. Standing together with our sons, his greatest achievements, we took turns releasing his ashes into the wind and watching them as they floated to the waters below.

EPILOGUE

I am now a surviving member of an exclusive club made up of those who experienced the exhilaration and terror of watching history unfold. We stood squarely as observers to something unique and often perplexing. To outsiders, in the absence of clear context, our experiences were a challenge to understand. Decades of passing time have changed the jargon; "urban guerrilla" has given way to "terrorist." History has been revised, and theories have been adjusted. And, of course, the players change.

The world is now painfully familiar with the idea of "Islamic fundamentalism." It is now called "Radical Islam." And, the world continues to confuse the events surrounding the Iranian revolution with the rise of terrorist offshoots of secular political groups, like ISIS wrapping itself in the false banner of religion to justify fascism.

Only those who, like me, experienced that time in Iran, understand me when I speak of sounds, smells, and feelings. They laugh and nod when I recall the way a vendor grasped the three bad fruits with the one good one. They smile knowingly at my stories of tracking down eggs or meat, of haggling for food by waving money in the face of the merchant.

It is a small club composed of those who braved the unfamiliarity of living among "foreigners" and never quite fitting in, desperately trying to assimilate while holding on to all that was good and true about "home."

Had the Islamic regime not arrested and murdered our friends, I would probably have returned to my life in Tehran and slipped back into the rhythm that I had created there for myself for as long as I was able to do so.

I like to believe that I would have just carried on—content to raise my children. Giving in to the time-consuming ways, frustrated by the inefficiency but appreciating the slowed pace of it all. I now muse that I would have eventually found that balance between my American ways and adopted culture.

Our other two sons would have been born there as well, and each boy would have been raised in the proud traditions of those whose names are hyphenated to proudly declare that they are both Iranian and American.

I came to live in Iran with a very specific political viewpoint that was naïve, based in hope and faith that people would somehow see the world as Hadj and I had hoped it would be. I had no true understanding of what a complete social insurrection would entail. I did not fully grasp the violence inherent in revolution. I did not see that it would touch me as it did.

I never got to live out my master plan to have my own home in Iran. I never got to raise my sons among many cousins. I never got to learn how to read Farsi and to speak without an accent. Along with Hadj, I mourned the murders of our comrades and friends. I mourned his life sentence of imposed exile from the country he loved. I cannot tell whether our marriage would have survived had we been able to return to Iran. I strongly believe that Hadj would have died with his comrades. I believe I would have been placed on a plane and sent away with our son.

I sit alone sometimes, trying to recall the sounds. I will be hit by a smell, a flavor, and be carried back to those days. My mind wanders back, and I see them all, the whole cast of characters, just as they were then. I will continue to tell my stories, disjointed, contradictory, and digressive, until the day I die. Certainly, time and age and maturity have affected my memories. So be it. I was there. I saw it. And now I have written it down.

It has taken me four decades to do so. Earlier it was too painful. The memories of our fallen friends were still vivid, painful and clear. It would have been presumptuous of me at that time to think I could recount my tale or to think that my story would have any significance. My experiences paled in comparison to the sacrifices those people made—and the ultimate price they paid.

And then life just got in the way. I continued to tell my stories to anyone who would listen. The Iranian expatriates and I reminisce about the old days. We analyze the news and share opinions of current events. They are now where I was then—cast out, unable to return, seeking comfort in the shared experiences of others. We form a strange fraternity of sorts. Our bond is our memories of what was and is now forever changed. We could now conceivably return to that country without incident. But, not one of us wishes to risk the heartache or the heartbreak of seeing today's reality. The hopes and dreams we held so dear to our hearts have been well and truly dashed.

I believe now my mission is to preach the words of my love for the country with as much truth and detail as I can muster. It was certainly not an easy place to live. Things were difficult and often the people were maddening. I was there, however, in the middle of something huge. The Iranian Revolution was not an event that took place over a week, a month, or even a year. There was no single day that marked its beginning or end.

Each day I turn to the news, anxious to see what has now become of that hostility once so palpable between the United States and Iran. The players change, new threats are exchanged. Elections are held while the people begin again to demand freedoms that they previously dared not seek. Bombs are dropped and players killed.

I bore others with my evangelical desires to answer that insidious rhetorical question, "Why do they hate us?" My response is always loud and emphatic: "They do not hate us."

I have been asked by many women in the United States whether I was always free to leave with my son. At the time of our unintentional exile, Betty Mahmoody, another American woman, wrote a book about her experiences called *Not Without My Daughter*. It was made into a movie with Sally Field playing the main character and I found the tone and tenor of the film both insulting and inaccurate.

As a divorce lawyer today, I know that both men and women marry abusive spouses all the time, all over the world. It is not uncommon. But that book and the subsequent film created a stereotype that to this day continues to haunt me.

No, my husband did not oppress me. None of the husbands of my American friends oppressed them. Yes, some American women were disliked by their in-laws. Yes, some of those women, in turn, found their in-laws to be conservative and narrow-minded. Yes, some American brides were forced to choose between leaving the country and taking their children with them. Yes, it is horrible that a man must grant his wife permission to leave the country with their children.

But one woman's experiences cannot be designated the norm. I met scores of American wives who had lived for over a decade in Iran since well before the revolution. They loved the country. They laughed at the "death to America" chants and told their relatives back home not to worry. They held jobs. They raised children. They lived, as I did, among the people. They spoke Farsi with no accent and knew the origins of all of the traditions. They celebrated Christmas and *No Ruz* with equal abandon. They were citizens, and they inspired me to become one as well.

So are there inequalities and outdated laws? Of course. But they are pebbles in the rice that is a stunningly beautiful and rich culture that welcomed me—and many others—with love.